CHEVY CORVETTE TRIVIA BOOK

Uncover The History & Facts Every Corvette Fan Needs To Know!

By

Seth Collins

Bridge Press
support@bridgepress.org

Please consider writing a review!
Just visit: purplelink.org/review

Copyright 2021. Dale Raynes. All Rights Reserved.
No part of this book may be reproduced or transmitted in any form or by any means, electronic or mechanical, including photocopying, recording or by any other form without written permission from the publisher.

ISBN: 978-1-955149-20-4

Acknowledgements:

Thank you to my beautiful wife for embracing my crazy love for this car!

TABLE OF CONTENTS

Introduction 1

Chapter 1: History and Origins 3
    Trivia Time! 3
    Answers 8
    Did You Know? 10

Chapter 2: Early Models 1953 - 1982 13
    Trivia Time! 13
    Answers 18
    Did You Know? 20

Chapter 3: Later Models 1983 - 2021 23
    Trivia Time! 23
    Answers 28
    Did You Know? 30

Chapter 4: Body Changes 33
    Trivia Time! 33
    Answers 38
    Did You Know? 40

Chapter 5: Corvette Records 43
    Trivia Time! 43
    Answers 48
    Did You Know? 50

Chapter 6: Corvette Speed 53
    Trivia Time! 53
    Answers 59
    Did You Know? 60

Chapter 7: Famous Drivers 63
    Trivia Time! 63
    Answers 68
    Did You Know? 69

Chapter 8: Famous Uses of Corvettes in Media 72
    Trivia Time! 72
    Answers 77
    Did You Know? 79

Chapter 9: Collections 82
    Trivia Time! 82
    Answers 87
    Did You Know? 89

Chapter 10: The Founders 92
Trivia Time! 92
Answers 97
Did You Know? 99

Chapter 11: Corvette Racing History 103
Trivia Time! 103
Answers 108
Did You Know? 110

Chapter 12: Corvette Specs 113
Trivia Time! 113
Answers 119
Did You Know? 121

Chapter 13: Rare Corvettes 124
Trivia Time! 124
Answers 130
Did You Know? 132

Chapter 14: Corvette Paint Colors 135
Trivia Time! 135
Answers 140
Did You Know? 142

Chapter 15: Random Facts 145

Trivia Time! 145

Answers 150

Did You Know? 152

Chapter 16: Corvettes, Crimes, and Accidents 155

Trivia Time! 155

Answers 160

Did You Know? 161

Chapter 17: What in the World? 164

Trivia Time! 164

Answers 170

Did You Know? 172

Chapter 18: US Road Facts 174

Trivia Time! 174

Answers 179

Did You Know? 180

INTRODUCTION

Corvettes have been a staple of American vehicles and society, from rare models to the more commonly issued and everything in between. Collectors and car enthusiasts love this iconic vehicle. First created in 1953, Corvette has been a symbol of freedom, youth, and speed, especially during the 1960s when these cars were the "it" car. Corvettes have been featured in songs, movies, and TV shows, furthering their importance in American culture.

This guide will ask questions such as "What year had the highest purchase rate?" to "What is the most popular color?" Hint: the answer is a three-letter word! Do you have what it takes to be a true Corvette fan?

Full of fun trivia and facts that will test any true Corvette fan, this guide covers decades of information about this iconic American car, such as who originally designed the Corvette and what year it was first produced. Test your knowledge with this guide, and see if you have what it takes to know nearly 70 years of Corvette history.

Whether you are an avid Corvette collector or know a few facts, this guide has something for everyone! If you're interested in the history of General Motors and its marketing strategies, the mechanical aspects of what makes a Corvette different from any other sports car out there, or the significance of Corvettes in American and international popular culture, this book will keep you and your friends entertained for pages and pages. From the C1 to the C8, we have enough Corvette history to get your engines running.

Each chapter of this guide covers different sections of Corvette history with trivia questions and a bonus "Did You Know?" section that gives detailed answers! These facts are ideal for any enthusiast or new Corvette fan; you might even learn new facts about your favorite car!

Think you are a Corvette enthusiast? Test your knowledge with this fun and informative guide and test your friends and see who knows the most! This guide is an excellent addition to any Corvette collection, and we promise it will take up less room than a real car!

Pick your favorite Corvette model, and let's get started!

CHAPTER 1:
HISTORY AND ORIGINS

TRIVIA TIME!

1. What year was the first Corvette model created?
    a. 1952
    b. 1953
    c. 1954
    d. 1955

2. True or False: The first Corvettes were created in Flint, Michigan.

3. What was the only year that a Corvette was not produced?
    a. 1981
    b. 1982
    c. 1983
    d. 1984

4. How much did the first Corvette cost in 1953?
    a. $3,490
    b. $4,490
    c. $5,490
    d. $6,490

5. True or False: Corvette got its name from a small warship.

6. What cylinder engine did the first C1 corvette have?
   a. 3 – Cylinder
   b. 5 – Cylinder
   c. 6 – Cylinder
   d. 8 – Cylinder

7. True or False: The original logo had a checkered flag and a red flag with Fleur-de-lis.

8. In what year were the most Corvettes sold?
   a. 1977
   b. 1978
   c. 1979
   d. 1980

9. What generation Corvette introduced pop-up headlamps and a removable roof panel?
   a. Generation C2
   b. Generation C3
   c. Generation C4

10. True or False: "Project Opel" was the secret title given to Corvette before it was released!

11. How many years was the C3 - 3Rd generation Corvette produced?

    a. 11
    b. 12
    c. 13
    d. 14

12. Why did Corvette get rid of the American flag logo in 1953?

    a. American flags were banned from commercial products.
    b. Corvette was not an American company.
    c. Red was not a common color of logos.
    d. The stripes of the American flag would have been distracting.

13. What year had the lowest sales since 1962?

    a. 1968
    b. 1969
    c. 1970
    d. 1971

14. True or False: There are no records of the very first Corvette from 1953.

15. What wood was used to mold fiberglass around during the first productions?

    a. Oak
    b. Mahogany
    c. Cherry
    d. Maple

16. How was Corvette spelled in the January 1953 press release?

    a. CoUrvette
    b. CorveTe
    c. CrVette
    d. CorvetteY

17. True or False: The first five Corvettes to be produced had outside rear-view mirrors.

18. What was the main reason for GM wanting to create Corvette?

    a. GM wanted to compete with European cars.
    b. Harley Earl wanted his own personal car.
    c. GM wanted a faster car than Ford.
    d. The design won a contest.

19. How many pieces of fiberglass were used with the original Corvette model?

    a. 26 pieces
    b. 36 pieces
    c. 46 pieces
    d. 56 pieces

20. True or False: GM executives were worried about using fiberglass.

ANSWERS

1. B – 1953
2. True
3. C – 1983
4. A – $3,490
5. True
6. C – 6 – Cylinder
7. False – The original logo was checkered flag with a stars and stripes flag, the American flag.
8. C – 1979
9. B – C3
10. True
11. D – 14
12. A – American flags were banned from commercial products.
13. C – 1970 ; only 17,316 units were sold.
14. True - There are no records of the vehicle.
15. B – Mahogany
16. A – CoUrvette
17. False – There were not outside rear-view mirrors.

18. A – GM wanted to compete with European cars.

19. C – 46 pieces

20. True

DID YOU KNOW?

- Myron Scott, chief Chevrolet photographer, suggested the name Corvette, based on a 17th century type of warship. These ships were smaller, faster, and stronger than other warships– just like Corvettes.

- During the first year of production, the first 300 Corvettes were created in Flint, Michigan. The first Corvette was produced on June 30, 1953. The car was hand-assembled with a Polo White exterior and red interiors.

- When the first Corvettes were created in 1953, only VIPs were able to purchase them. This included mayors, governors, and celebrities. Not a single Chevrolet dealership in 1953 received a Corvette, yet the rich elites were not interested, and many of the Corvettes never sold. This threatened the continuation production of the vehicle, and it was nearly discontinued.

- Hours before the Motorama NYC show in January 1953, the Corvette logo had to be changed. The original logo was a checkered flag and an American flag, but the designer learned that it was illegal to have an American flag on commercial products. The American flag was changed to a French Fleur-de-lis, a reflection of the French etymology of the Chevrolet name!

- The French fleur-de-lis is a symbol for purity and translates to "lily flower" in French. It is sometimes also called a flower-de-luce.
- When the first Corvette was shown at the Motorama NYC show it was during the McCarthy era of fear. This resulted in General Motors installing hidden tape recorders inside the car to listen to potential buyers and guests.
- While helpful to hear customer feedback, it was how GM learned that Ford Motors was also spying. It was heard that Ford engineers and planners were discussing the car's design, and it was no surprise when the "spies" created the Ford Thunderbird a year later.
- One of the first Corvette prototypes was carved from Philippine mahogany wood into the exact shape of the parts and used as prototypes. These parts were later used in the production of Corvettes.
- The Corvette's body was composed of 46 pieces of fiberglass. It was used to save weight, and it also allowed for designers to create better curves and rounded shapes. This was due to the fiberglass being stamped out with a steel press.
- The mahogany was carved using a semi-permanent tool. The fiberglass was placed on the wood and

shaped the model. None of these wood carvings remain, only photos.

- The GM executives worried about the choice of fiberglass. Harley Earl assured that the choice was the best option. Fiberglass was not used in mass-market vehicles, and this option could have been risky.
- In January 1953, the man behind the press release would misspell Corvette. The error was caught and has never been published in a book or magazine.
- The only parts of the 1953 Corvettes that were originally created for the new car was the fiberglass body. The rest of the parts were already made- with Chevrolet parts!
- 1979 sold the most units of Corvettes, with 53,807 Corvettes created that year!

CHAPTER 2:
EARLY MODELS 1953 - 1982

TRIVIA TIME!

1. What city had the first full-scale Corvette displayed at a hotel in 1953?
    a. Los Angeles
    b. Miami
    c. New York City
    d. Bowling Green

2. True or False: The first Corvette windows could not roll down.

3. In what three cities have Corvette cars been manufactured?
    a. Flint, St. Louis, and Bowling Green
    b. Detroit, Cleveland, and Indianapolis
    c. St. Louis, Little Rock, and Flint
    d. Bowling Green, Memphis, and Cincinnati

4. True or False: Corvette was the first vehicle to create a real "wrap-around" windshield.

5. In what year was the first coupe and convertible Corvette made?
   a. 1959
   b. 1960
   c. 1963
   d. 1965

6. True or False: The color "Inca Silver" acrylic lacquer paint was used for multiple years.

7. How long did it take the 1953 Corvette to go from 0 to 60 mph?
   a. 10 seconds
   b. 11 seconds
   c. 12 seconds
   d. 13 seconds

8. The first Corvettes were made out of this material:
   a. Fiberglass
   b. Aluminum
   c. Steel
   d. Iron

9. How much did the 1953 original Corvette sell for?
   a. $2,498
   b. $3,498
   c. $4,498
   d. $5,498

10. What was the only year that the split rear window was produced?
    a. 1959
    b. 1961
    c. 1963
    d. 1965

11. True or False: 1979 was the only year that a Chevy Vega 4 spoke designer steering wheel was used.

12. What color was *not* used in 1954?
    a. Pennant Blue
    b. Sportsman Red
    c. Sunshine Yellow
    d. Polo White

13. How many Corvettes were produced in 1955?
    a. 700
    b. 1700
    c. 2700
    d. 3700

14. In the first year that AC was offered, how much did it cost?
    a. $221
    b. $321
    c. $421
    d. $521

15. True or False: The 1965 396-V8-engine Corvette was one of the fastest cars on the market.

16. What was the first year that a side mounted exhaust system was used?
    a. 1965
    b. 1967
    c. 1969
    d. 1980

17. True or False: In 1956-58 a limited number of Corvettes had a Conelrad radio system.

18. How did designer Harley Earl deal with foggy head and taillights?
    a. Dual-walled glass
    b. Automatic spray
    c. Holes in the glass
    d. Small internal wipers

19. Which of these nicknames *was not used* for the C2 Corvette?
    a. Batmobile
    b. Mako Shark
    c. Sting Ray
    d. Fightermobile

20. What was the name of the wooden mockup Model C2 that was used for Caltech wind tunnel experiments?
    a. Venus Rabbit
    b. Jupiter Bear
    c. Space Buck
    d. Apollo Horse

21. What was the last year that Corvette offered "Wide Whitewall" tires?

   a. 1958
   b. 1959
   c. 1960
   d. 1961

22. True or False: The original dashboards were made out of leather and wood.

23. In which year did Corvette have only an automatic transmission?

   a. 1978
   b. 1980
   c. 1982
   d. 1984

24. True or False: First-generation Corvettes had the option of coupes or convertibles.

ANSWERS

1. C – New York City, at the Walldorf Astoria Hotel.
2. True – The windows had to be taken out, in order to have the windows down!
3. A – Flint, St. Louis, and Bowling Green
4. True
5. C – 1963
6. False – It was only used in 1959.
7. B – 11 seconds
8. A – Fiberglass
9. B – $3,498 or $31,473 in modern day prices.
10. C – 1963
11. False – It was 1976
12. C – Sunshine yellow was not a color used.
13. A – 700
14. C – $421
15. True
16. A – 1965
17. False – It was between spring 1953-54.
18. A – Duel-walled glass

19. D – Fightermobile

20. C – Space Buck

21. D – 1961

22. True

23. C – 1982

24. False – Only convertibles were offered.

DID YOU KNOW?

- At the GM Motorama traveling car show, a 1953 Corvette was placed on display. This was one of the first times the public saw a Corvette. The first produced Corvette was not ready for six months after the reveal. At the same show, the Buick Wildcat, Oldsmobile Starfire, and Cadillac Orleans were shown. Dancers, singers, and an orchestra were hired to perform at the show!

- Due to electrical grounding problems with the fiberglass bodies, the first generation 1953 Corvettes could not be "rolled" off the production line. Employees had to manually push the cars off the line!

- Besides not having roll down windows, the first model did not have exterior handles. In order to open the door, you'd have to use the internal handle. Windows were made from plastic curtains and buyers had the option for AM radio and a heater.

- In 1958 the Corvette underwent interior and exterior changes; the exterior changes were some of the most noticeable. Designers added two extra headlights, additional chrome accents, and added louver to the hood. This design was changed the next year.

- When the C2 generation of Corvettes were designed, they were based on the 1959 Sting Ray race car. GM Vice President of Styling Bill Mitchell drove a Sting Ray and it was designed in honor of the VP.

- The 1963 Stingray was the first coupe with a convertible roof top. The new engine, design, and technology led this Corvette to be desirable. The independent rear suspension system was advanced for the time– the split rear window was only done in 1963!

- The split rear window would cause arguments between GM Vice President Bill Mitchell and engineer Zora Arkus-Duntov. Mitchell wanted to have a split rear window, and Arkus-Duntov felt that it would block rear vision. The rear split window would only be manufactured in 1963, before production stopped it.

- Many car enthusiasts know that the Chevy Vega 4, produced between 1970 to 1977, was a near failure. The car was an aluminum, black engine and "guzzled" oil. The car was reported to have valve leaks and cracks, and some of the engines even caught on fire and overheated! In 1976, Corvette would take the steering wheel and use it for that production year!

- In 1954, only 3,460 units were produced following the lack of sales the year before. Four colors were offered: pennant blue, sportsman red, black, and polo white.

- After two years of poor sales and many unsold 1954 Corvettes, only 700 Corvettes were produced in 1955.

- One of the ways to know where the original Corvettes were created is to look at the VIN tag. VINs starting with E53F were crated in Flint, Michigan, while VINs that start with E54S were created in St. Louis, Missouri.

- In 1951, the first national emergency broadcast system was created: the Conelrad National Defense System. A small number of C1 Corvettes were created with this radio system, before the radio Emergency Alert System was created.

- Condensation would cause foggy head and taillights, creating a danger for early Corvette Drivers. Harley Earl would create a dual-walled glass system that allowed for airflow that dealt with the changing temperatures. This helped prevent dimming of the light and fogging!

- In 1982, Corvette only had automatic transmissions and did not offer manual transmissions even by special order.

CHAPTER 3:
LATER MODELS 1983 - 2021

TRIVIA TIME!

1. In what year did Corvette move production to Bowling Green, Kentucky?
    a. 1975
    b. 1977
    c. 1981
    d. 1983

2. True or False: The Corvette 4th Generation in 1984 was designed by Dave McLellan.

3. How much did the 1984 Corvette sell for?
    a. $19,800
    b. $20,800
    c. $21,800
    d. $22,800

4. True or False: In 1984 the convertible top was reintroduced!

5. What speed did the ZRI reach when trying to break the fastest car record in 1990?

    a. 165 mph
    b. 175 mph
    c. 185 mph
    d. 205 mph

6. How many people bought the ZR1 Corvette in 1990?

    a. 3,000
    b. 5,000
    c. 7,000
    d. 9,000

7. True or False: Corvette partnered with Group Lotus to try and create the fastest car.

8. In what year did the pop-headlights end?

    a. 1998
    b. 2000
    c. 2002
    d. 2004

9. What was the style cue that was included in the C4 Corvette's design?

    a. "Pepsi Bottle"
    b. "Coke Bottle"
    c. "Whale Tail"
    d. "Whitewalls"

10. In 1990, the most expensive Corvette to date was created. How much did it sell for?

   a. $38,995
   b. $48,995
   c. $58,995
   d. $68,995

11. True or False: 2020 marks the start of the newest generation of Corvettes: C8.

12. What year was the Head-Up display option offered?

   a. 1990
   b. 1994
   c. 1995
   d. 1998

13. How many Corvettes were produced in 2020?

   a. 20,368
   b. 25,368
   c. 30,368
   d. 35,368

14. True or False: You could buy a Corvette without an engine in 1987.

15. What was the first year that all Corvette parts were made exclusively for Corvettes?

   a. 1980
   b. 1987
   c. 1990
   d. 1997

16. Between which years was the black exterior color not offered?

    a. 1970 to 1976
    b. 1965 to 1969
    c. 1971 to 1980
    d. 1969 to 1978

17. How many hours did it take to build the C5 Corvette?

    a. 35 hours
    b. 45 hours
    c. 55 hours
    d. 65 hours

18. In what year did the first Corvette to retail for over $100,000?

    a. 2000
    b. 2005
    c. 2007
    d. 2009

19. To celebrate the 25th anniversary, Corvette added what to the vehicle?

    a. Fastback rear end
    b. Updated steering wheel
    c. Changed side exhaust
    d. Updated doors

20. True or False: The new C5 Corvettes continued with the tradition of painting the first 200 produced of the new generation in white!

21. What year saw the return of the Grand Sport Corvette?

    a. 2015
    b. 2016
    c. 2017
    d. 2018

22. Where is the engine located in the 2020 C8 Corvette?

    a. Front
    b. Middle
    c. Rear

ANSWERS

1. C – 1981
2. True – Dave McLellan became the chief of design in 1975.
3. C – $21,800
4. False – It was reintroduced in 1986.
5. B – 175 mph
6. A – 3,000
7. True
8. D – 2004
9. B – "Coke Bottle"
10. C – $58,995
11. True
12. D – 1998
13. A – 20,368
14. True
15. D – 1997
16. A – 1970 to 1976
17. C – 55 hours
18. D – 2009; it was the 2009 ZR1.

19. A – Fastback Rear End

20. False – This generation broke the tradition and painted the first 200 red!

21. C – 2017

22. B – Middle

DID YOU KNOW?

- The first generation of Corvettes were built in Flint, Michigan, from 1954 to 1981. They were produced in Saint Louis, Missouri. In 1982, the production of Corvettes was moved to Bowling Green, Kentucky, where they are made today!

- When "Father of the Corvette" Zora Arkus-Duntov retired in 1975, Dave McLellan became the new chief of design. McLellan would keep the design the same until 1984 when he redesigned and changed the car. This marked the 4th generation Corvette.

- The newly designed Generation 4 moved away from the traditional Sting Ray style of the previous generation. The frame was changed, with body panels and bumpers made out of plastic modeling rather than fiberglass to create a streamline style.

- The newly designed Dave McLellan Corvette was the first time since 1963 that a Corvette was completely redesigned!

- The new exterior design for the C4 Corvettes saw the removal of the "Coke Bottle" design, which refers to the pinched sides near the passenger area. This looked similar to the glass Coke bottle design.

- For 11 years, the convertible top on Corvettes was on a hiatus, until it was reintroduced in 1986. It was an extra $6,000 for the convertible. Included was also an Indy 500 plaque, after the 1986 yellow Corvette pace car at the Indy 500.

- The creation of the C4 Corvette saved Corvette; the old design was seen as boring, given that it had been produced for 14 years. The engine was heavy and slower than most racing cars and had less than 200 horsepower.

- In 1990 Corvette partnered with Group Lotus with the goal to create the fastest car, the ZR1 broke the record for fastest 24-hour, with speeds of 175 mph at the 24 hour-5,000-mile race. The car was built with 380 hp @ 6200 rpm, and a V8 engine.

- The 1990 Corvette was also the most expensive Corvette to date; it sold for $58,995.

- The Head-Up display was first introduced in 1998. The RPM, oil pressure, and speed gauge were displayed in the windshield!

- In 2020, Corvette produced 20,368 vehicles, with 16,787 Stingray Coupes and 3,581 Stingray Convertibles. This is half of the original production order, primarily because of factory shutdown due to the COVID-19 pandemic. It is likely that this year of Corvettes will be collectable in the future.

- Every Corvette until 1997 was made with other Chevrolet parts, not exclusively made with Corvette parts. 1997 was the first year that nearly every part was created for Corvettes, with the exception of the exterior door handles– those were the same as the Oldsmobile Aurora.

- When the first C5 Corvettes were produced, the production time was dropped from 70 hours with the C4 to 55 hours!

- In 2017, Corvette returned the iconic Grand Sport design in the Corvette C7 Grand Sport. This design was similar to the 1996 C4 model! It was also a tribute to engineer Zora Arkus-Duntov– this can be seen in the near domed back rear windows.

- For the first time in Corvette history, the engine is being moved; the 2020 C8 Corvette now has the engine located in the middle of the vehicle. Many other speed cars have already made the change, such as the Ferrari 488, Lamborghini Huracán, and Audi R8!

CHAPTER 4:
BODY CHANGES

TRIVIA TIME!

1. True or False: Designer Bill Mitchell was inspired by a Mako shark for the Sting Ray.

2. What year did Corvette stop using its original color of Polo White?
    a. 1954
    b. 1955
    c. 1956
    d. 1957

3. In what year was the V8 engine introduced?
    a. 1955
    b. 1956
    c. 1953
    d. 1954

4. True or False: The 2020 Corvette was the first time the engine was allocated to the back of vehicle.

5. Between 1963 and 1967, Corvette had an option for what size gas tank?

   a. 20 gallons
   b. 26 gallons
   c. 30 gallons
   d. 36 gallons

6. True or False: Seatbelts have always been installed in Corvettes.

7. What luxury amenity was not included in 1963?

   a. Power Steering
   b. Air Conditioning
   c. Leather Seats
   d. Sun Visors

8. How many vertical bars, or "teeth," were on the grill of the 1956 Corvette?

   a. 12
   b. 13
   c. 14
   d. 15

9. True or False: Between 1963 and 1982, there was no opening trunk for storage.

10. In 1954, three new colors were offered. Which color *was not* offered?

   a. Yellow
   b. Red
   c. Blue
   d. Black

11. What amenity did the 1956 Corvette *not* include?

   a. External door handles
   b. Power-operated folding roof
   c. Air conditioning
   d. Windows that rolled down

12. True or False: Changed fuel injection made the 1957 a faster and more desirable vehicle.

13. In what year did the National Highway and Traffic Safety Association require cars to have front and rear bumpers?

   a. 1970
   b. 1971
   c. 1972
   d. 1973

14. What changes were seen after the 1973 Corporate Average Fuel Economy laws were passed?

   a. Fuel economy standards were created.
   b. All cars were required to run on diesel.
   c. The gas cap location was changed.
   d. More emission from cars were created.

15. In what year did Corvette re-introduce Stingray, one word.
    a. 1984
    b. 1994
    c. 2004
    d. 2014

16. In what year was keyless car entry introduced?
    a. 2000
    b. 2003
    c. 2005
    d. 2007

17. What is the *most popular* external Corvette color?
    a. Jet Black
    b. Torch Red
    c. Accelerate Yellow
    d. Arctic White

18. What is the *least popular* external Corvette color?
    a. Jet Black
    b. Torch Red
    c. Accelerate Yellow
    d. Arctic White

19. True or False: The 2020 Corvette Stingray has a "Fly Car" mode.

20. What was one of the ways that enabled the 1963 Grand Sport to weigh less than other models?

   a. Fiberglass panels were half the thickness
   b. Changed wheel sizes
   c. Small body shape
   d. Bumpers made of thinner material

21. How many separate hoods did the 1967 Corvette have?

   a. One
   b. Two
   c. Three
   d. Four

ANSWERS

1. True – Bill Mitchell was deep sea fishing when he caught a Mako shark. This was his inspiration behind the String Ray Corvette!

2. D – 1957

3. A – 1955

4. True

5. D – 36-gallon gas tank

6. False

7. D – Sun visors were including in 1958!

8. B – 13 "teeth"

9. True

10. A – Yellow

11. C – Air Conditioning

12. True

13. B – 1971

14. A – Fuel economy standards were created.

15. D – 2014

16. C – 2005

17. B – Torch Red

18. C – Accelerate Yellow

19. True

20. A - Fiberglass panels were half the thickness

21. C – Three

DID YOU KNOW?

- When designing the new second generation to be released in 1963, designer Bill Mitchell caught a shark while deep sea fishing. The Mako shark that was caught would influence his design; this new Corvette was named Sting Ray.

- In 2014, Corvette re-introduced the name of Stingray; the name was slightly changed from two words into one.

- It was rumored that early prototypes were painted to match shark skin color.

- When the V8 engine was installed, Chevrolet engineer Zora Arkus-Duntov pushed for the switch. This created better performance and gave credibility to Corvettes which would increase the demand for it in 1955. This new engine was able to reach 240 horsepower and 265 CID small blocks.

- 1980 Federal mandates required that Corvette speedometers cap at 85 mph. This was done to help stop street racing and help deal with the gas crisis.

- Factory-installed seatbelts were not installed in the Corvette until 1958. It was not until 1968 that seat beats were federally required in vehicles!

- In 1956, the Corvette underwent a complete change, the first major change since the car was introduced in

1953. New features included external door handles, windows that rolled into the door panel, and a power-operated folding convertible roof.

- The 1956 Corvette was inspired by Mercedes-Benz 300SL coupe– the scalloped sides are similar.

- Most cars in the 1950s had carburetors, and engineer Zora Arkus-Duntov wanted to make a faster and better preforming Corvette. Changing the fuel injection allowed for more horsepower, 290 HP, and created a more sought-after vehicle on the market.

- In 1971, the National Highway and Traffic Safety Associated required all cars produced after 1973 to have a front and rear bumper that could withstand being hit at 5mph. The new requirement left vehicles with heavy bumpers, an additional 60-100 lbs. New laws also changed the size of the front end, and the door pillar size in vehicles.

- In 1973, the Corporate Average Fuel Economy set new annual fuel economy standards in passenger cars. This required engineers to increase fuel efficiency, thereby decreasing emission in cars.

- In 2005, keyless entry was first introduced. That same year, pop-up headlights were not included; it was the first time since 1962.

- The most popular Corvette color is Torch Red with 25% of Corvettes sold being in that color. The least popular options are both Accelerate Yellow and

Zeus Bronze, as these two colors are only used on 3% Corvettes.

- The "Flying Car" mode uses the Corvette Performance Traction Management system– the wheels stay off the ground and spin faster with no resistance. A system senses the wheels and will lift the vehicle's wheels off the ground.

- 1967 was the first time that Corvette had three hoods: a small block hood, a big block hood, and a L-88 hood.

CHAPTER 5:
CORVETTE RECORDS

TRIVIA TIME!

1. What speed did the fastest Corvette reach?

    a. 204 mph
    b. 207 mph
    c. 212 mph
    d. 223 mph

2. What is the highest selling year for Corvette?

    a. 1975 Corvette
    b. 1977 Corvette
    c. 1979 Corvette
    d. 1781 Corvette

3. True or False: Corvette is the longest-running continuous production of a passenger car!

4. What is the most expensive Corvette ever sold?

    a. $3.75 million
    b. $3.85 million
    c. $3.95 million
    d. $4.05 million

5. In 1979, the highest number of Corvettes were sold. How many were sold?
   a. 48,423
   b. 50,342
   c. 51,965
   d. 53,807

6. True or False: The 1999 the Corvette Convertible was awarded Best Engineered Car of the 20th Century.

7. In what year did the first Corvette reach 200 mph?
   a. 2009
   b. 2011
   c. 2013
   d. 2014

8. What speed did the Corvette Stingray reach in 2014 while going in reverse?
   a. 33 mph
   b. 43 mph
   c. 53 mph
   d. 63 mph

9. True or False: To celebrate the 250,000th produced Corvette in 1969, it was painted silver.

10. What year did Corvette hit one million produced vehicles?

    a. 1982
    b. 1992
    c. 1990
    d. 1980

11. True or False: Zora Arkus-Duntov drove the Chevrolet Sudan to set new a class record in 1955.

12. How long did it take the 1960 Corvette to reach the summit of Pikes Peak– 4,303 meters?

    a. 17 minutes
    b. 19 minutes
    c. 22 minutes
    d. 24 minutes

13. True or False: As of 2012, one third of all sports cars sold in the United States are Corvettes.

14. Which car is the fastest Corvette in history?

    a. 1990 ZR-1
    b. 1968 LT-2
    c. 1972 XP-895
    d. 1969 ZL-1

15. How many international speed records did the ZR-1, the 1990 Corvette, set?

    a. Zero
    b. Three
    c. Seven
    d. Eleven

16. What was the first race that Corvette Racing raced in 1999?

    a. Daytona 24 Hours
    b. 24 Hours at Le Mans
    c. Sebring 24 Hour
    d. Indianapolis 500

17. True or False: Corvette Racing was the first professional sports car racing in North America to win 100 worldwide races.

18. How many times has Corvette produced over 40,000 vehicles in a year?

    a. One
    b. Ten
    c. Fifteen
    d. Twenty

19. How much did this rare 1967 Corvette L88 sell for at auction in 2021?

    a. $1.69 million
    b. $2.69 million
    c. $3.69 million
    d. $4.69 million

20. What year was Corvette was awarded "North American Car of the Year" at the North American International Auto Show?

    a. 1995
    b. 1996
    c. 1997
    d. 1998

ANSWERS

1. C – 212 mph; it was the Corvette ZR1.
2. C – 1979
3. True
4. B – $3.85 million
5. D – 53,807 units
6. True – The Society of Automotive Engineer gave this award.
7. A – 2009
8. C – 53 mph
9. False – It was painted gold!
10. B – 1992
11. True – Zora Arkus-Duntov was the driver.
12. A – 17 minutes (17 minutes and 24.05 seconds)
13. True
14. B – 1968 LT-2
15. C – Seven International Records
16. A – Daytona 24 Hour
17. True
18. A – Once, in 2007

19. B- $3.69 million

20. D - 1998

DID YOU KNOW?

- In 2019, the Corvette ZR1 hit speeds of 212 mph. This was the fastest speed a Corvette had ever reached.

- The most expensive Corvette sold was a Chevy Corvette L88 Coupe. It sold for $3.85 million at a 2014 auction. Only 20 of these models were ever built!

- It was the ZR1 that first reached 200 mph in 2009. The ZR1 also hit the fastest speed of 212 mph in 2019!

- While Corvette has the record for the longest-running continuous production of a passenger car, it is not the longest running vehicle production– the Chevrolet Suburban is!

- Summit Pikes Peak in Colorado helped launch Corvette into the new world of racing. Zora Arkus-Duntov drove a new 1956 Corvette and raced it in the sedan class. Because the car was unreleased, they camouflaged it with painting stripes to stop competitors from seeing the unreleased car during the race.

- Arkus-Duntov reached the summit in 17 minutes and 24 seconds and set a sedan class record. Corvette used this win and record for advertisements.

- Zora Arkus-Duntov used two 1956 Chevrolet 210s: two and four door sedans. with 256 cubic inch small-blocks, V-8 engines, three-speed manual transmissions, and a 4.55 rear end. These modifications were able to help the car set a new record, as Arkus-Duntov raced it up 4,720 feet in elevation gain.

- The 1968 LT-2 was created as a protype design for the 1970 Corvette. This car would be the fastest Corvette *ever* created. Going from 0-60 mph in 2.8 seconds, modern 2020 Corvettes can reach that speed in 2.9 seconds.

- The first race that the newly formed Corvette racing entered was the Daytona 24 Hours on February 5, 1999! Their first win was at the Texas Motor Speedway on September 2, 2000!

- Corvette Racing would be the first North American professional race team to win 100 worldwide wins, with 18 different drivers winning the races. Famed drivers Oliver Gavin has won the most at 50, Johnny O'Connell with 41, and Jan Magnussen at 35 wins!

- 1984 saw the second biggest production of Corvettes with 51,547 vehicles made. Since that iconic year, Corvette has only produced over 40,000 once, in 2007.

- In March 2021, a rare Sunfire Yellow Corvette was sold for $2,695,000 million. This 1967 Corvette L88 was one of twenty built that year. In 2013, the same model, but in Candy Apple Red, sold for $3.4 million at auction.

- In 1998, Automotive Media voted Corvette the "North American Car of the Year" at the North American International Auto Show.

- The last six cars produced during 1998 were painted in a special color of "Medium Purple Pearl Metallic." There were 396 cars painted in this color.

CHAPTER 6:
CORVETTE SPEED

TRIVIA TIME!

1. What was the top speed for the original 1953 Corvette?

    a. 100 mph
    b. 104 mph
    c. 106 mph
    d. 108 mph

2. What horsepower did the 1955 Corvette have?

    a. 145 horsepower
    b. 175 horsepower
    c. 195 horsepower
    d. 202 horsepower

3. How long did it take the 1958 Corvette to reach 0-60 mph?

    a. 9.2 seconds
    b. 9.4 seconds
    c. 9.6 seconds
    d. 9.8 seconds

4. What was the top speed that the 1961 Corvette could reach?

   a. 102 mph
   b. 105 mph
   c. 107 mph
   d. 109 mph

5. What year saw a Corvette with a speed of 0-60 mph in 5.9 seconds?

   a. 1960
   b. 1961
   c. 1962
   d. 1963

6. How long did it take the 1967 Corvette to reach 0-60 mph?

   a. 4.7 seconds
   b. 4.8 seconds
   c. 5.0 seconds
   d. 5.2 seconds

7. In what year did Corvette see one of the fastest engines?

   a. 1967
   b. 1968
   c. 1969
   d. 1970

8. What was the top speed that the 1970 Corvette reached?

   a. 140 mph
   b. 142 mph
   c. 144 mph
   d. 146 mph

9. What horsepower did the 1974 Corvette have?

   a. 195 horsepower
   b. 200 horsepower
   c. 205 horsepower
   d. 210 horsepower

10. How long did it take the 1978 Corvette to reach 0-60 mph?

    a. 7.2 seconds
    b. 7.6 seconds
    c. 7.8 seconds
    d. 8.0 seconds

11. What was the top speed of the 1984 Corvette?

    a. 140 mph
    b. 142 mph
    c. 146 mph
    d. 148 mph

12. How long did it take the 1989 Corvette to reach 0-60 mph?

    a. 6.4 seconds
    b. 6.6 seconds
    c. 6.8 seconds
    d. 7.0 seconds

13. In what year did Corvette have a top speed of 175 miles per hour?

    a. 1984
    b. 1986
    c. 1988
    d. 1990

14. How much horsepower did the 1993 Corvette have?

    a. 300 horsepower
    b. 305 horsepower
    c. 310 horsepower
    d. 315 horsepower

15. What was the top speed of the 1997 Corvette?

    a. 160 mph
    b. 165 mph
    c. 170 mph
    d. 175 mph

16. With a unique six-speed manual transmission, how fast could the 2002 Corvette reach 0-60 mph?

   a. 3.5 seconds
   b. 3.7 seconds
   c. 3.9 seconds
   d. 4.1 seconds

17. What was the top speed of the 2007 Corvette?

   a. 186 mph
   b. 188 mph
   c. 190 mph
   d. 192 mph

18. How much horsepower did the 2011 Corvette have?

   a. 420 hp
   b. 430 hp
   c. 440 hp
   d. 450 hp

19. What was the top speed of the 2015 Corvette?

   a. 2012
   b. 2013
   c. 2014
   d. 2015

20. What year did Corvette claim to have built the fastest model?

    a. 2017
    b. 2018
    c. 2019
    d. 2020

ANSWERS

1. D – 108 mph
2. C – 195 Horsepower
3. A – 9.2 seconds
4. D – 109 MPH
5. C - 1962
6. A – 4.7 seconds
7. B - 1968
8. C – 144 mph
9. A – 195 horsepower
10. C – 7.8 seconds
11. B – 142 mph
12. B – 6.6 seconds
13. D – 175 mph
14. A – 300 horsepower
15. D – 175 mph
16. C – 3.9 seconds
17. A – 186 mph
18. B – 430 hp
19. D – 2015
20. C - 2019

DID YOU KNOW?

- It would take the 1953 Corvette nearly 11 seconds to reach 0-60 mph! Within seven years Corvette engineers were able to drop that time by over four seconds.

- In 1955, the new "Turbo-Fire" Corvette with the V-8 engine was able to create one of the fastest Corvettes on the market at the time.

- Each year Corvette created fast cars, learning as they went, and 1967 was no different. This Corvette was able to reach 0-60 mph in 4.7 seconds, and 0-100 mph in 11.2 seconds. This car was also able to reach a top speed of 140 mph.

- One of the fastest Corvette motors was in the 1968 LT-2, which was the prototype for the 1970 model. The engine was placed in the body of a 1968 model and was able to reach speeds of 0-60 mph in 2.8 seconds.

- Even after the great performance in 1967, the following year saw a slower car with a 0-60 mph. This was due to the mandated emission equipment that added weight to the vehicle. This model also had 400 horsepower, while the year prior had 435 horsepower.

- Due to changing emissions regulations and safety equipment now required in vehicles, the 1973

Corvette was seeing much slower times than previous years. With a 0-60 mph time of 6.4 seconds, it was nearly one second slower than the year prior.

- Chevy had also changed from a SAE gross horsepower to a SAE net for the 1973 production. This drastically affected the horsepower and left it with only 275 hp.

- Starting in 1980, all Corvettes had to have a speedometer show the maximum speed of 85 miles per hour! This was done to try and slow drivers down and use less gas given the energy crisis of the 1970s.

- 1990 saw the introduction of the Corvette ZR-1. This model featured a 380 hp engine and could reach 0-60 mph in 4.5 seconds with a top speed of 175 mph! This model helped grow Corvette sales after fans were disappointed with the early C4 models.

- The 1993 Corvette had horsepower of 300 hp at 5,000 rpm and could reach 0-60 mph in 5.1 seconds!

- Described as "slippery," the 1997 Corvette reached impressive speeds, with a max speed of 175 mph. This car would debut the C5 generation Corvette.

- The 2002 Z06 Corvette would be built with a unique six-speed manual transmission. It was able to reach speeds of 0-60 mph in 3.9 seconds. The engineers of this car added 15 pounds-feet torque, which totaled 400 pounds-feet at 4,800 rpm. This helped add to the speed!

- The 2011 Grand Sport Corvette was able to reach a top speed of 185 mph and reach 0-60 mph in 4.2 seconds!
- In 2019, Corvette debuted the ZR1, which is the fastest and most powerful Corvette ever created. This vehicle has 755 horsepower and a 6.2-liter supercharged engine, with a top speed of 210 mph. It can reach 0-60 mph in 2.9 seconds!

CHAPTER 7:
FAMOUS DRIVERS

TRIVIA TIME!

1. True or False: Astronaut Alan Shepard was given a Corvette when he arrived back on Earth.

2. What colors did the 1969 astronauts order their Corvettes in?
    a. White and red
    b. Black and gold
    c. Blue and red
    d. Silver and black

3. What year did GM end their "free" Corvette program for astronauts?
    a. 1969
    b. 1970
    c. 1971
    d. 1972

4. Which celebrity actor considers a Corvette to be their car of choice?

    a. George Clooney
    b. Matt Damon
    c. Johnny Deep
    d. Brad Pitt

5. What color Corvette did Neil Armstrong buy following his Apollo 11 flight?

    a. Polo White
    b. Sportsman Red
    c. Black
    d. Marina Blue

6. True or False: John Fitch and Bob Grossman were the drivers at the 1960 24 Hours of Le Mans race

7. Briggs Cunningham's Corvette was introduced into the National Corvette Museum in what year?

    a. 1990
    b. 2004
    c. 2011
    d. 2019

8. What is the average age of a Corvette owner?

    a. 61
    b. 65
    c. 71
    d. 74

9. Long Island carpenter Dennis Amodeo won how many Corvettes in 1988?

   a. 26
   b. 30
   c. 36
   d. 40

10. True or False: Jerry Seinfeld drove a Cascade Green 1956 Corvette on his show *Comedians in Cars Getting Coffee*.

11. How many Corvettes does the largest Corvette dealership in the world have?

   a. 403
   b. 503
   c. 603
   d. 703

12. Drivers Bob Johnson and Dave Heinz placed *what* overall at Sebring race in 1973?

   a. 4th place
   b. 6th place
   c. 9th place
   d. 20th place

13. Who is John Powell to Corvette?

   a. Designer
   b. Creator of the Corvette Challenge
   c. Lead Engineer
   d. Protestor of Corvettes

14. This member of The Beatles owns a blue C5 convertible Corvette.

    a. Paul McCartney
    b. Ringo Starr
    c. George Harrison
    d. John Lennon

15. What year Corvette did Jerry Seinfeld drive on his show *Comedians in Cars Getting Coffee*?

    a. 1960
    b. 1961
    c. 1963
    d. 1965

16. True or False: A Corvette has been in an Academy Award winning movie.

17. How many wins has Corvette Racing driver Oliver Gavin won for Corvette?

    a. 40
    b. 50
    c. 60
    d. 70

18. True or False: Zora Arkus-Duntov invited Briggs Cunningham Jr. to drive Corvettes in the 1960s.

19. What year Corvette did Eric "Otter" Stratton drive in the film *Animal House* in 1978?

   a. 1955
   b. 1959
   c. 1965
   d. 1969

20. George Maharis and Martin Milner were stars of what TV show that had a Corvette?

   a. Route 66
   b. Route 81
   c. Route 67
   d. Route 55

ANSWERS

1. True – Alan Shepard was given a 1962 Corvette.
2. B – Black and Gold
3. C – 1971
4. A – George Clooney
5. D – Marina Blue
6. True
7. D – 2019
8. A – 61 years old
9. C – 36 Corvettes
10. True
11. B – 503 Corvettes
12. A – 4th place
13. B – Creator of the Corvette Challenge
14. A – Paul McCarthy
15. C – 1963
16. False
17. B – 50 wins
18. True
19. B – 1959
20. A – Route 66

DID YOU KNOW?

- Astronaut Alan Shepard had driven Corvettes prior to becoming a part of the Mercury 7 team. Shepard purchased a used 1953 and a used 1957 Corvette to celebrate becoming part of the space program. He was given clearance to race down the Langley Air Force Base runway, where he hit speeds of 100 mph.

- Three of the other Mercury 7 astronauts, Gus Grissom, Gordon Cooper, and Deke Slayton, were also given Corvettes as part of a deal with NASA. Each Corvette was leased for one dollar a year. They were given the nickname "Astro-Vettes," and the astronauts would race each other at Cape Canaveral! Chevrolet and NASA began a partnership where any astronaut could get a Corvette.

- In 1969, astronauts Alan Beam, Charles "Pete" Conrad, and Richard Gorden all ordered their Corvettes to have custom gold and black exterior. This was done to match their lunar module spacecraft.

- Drivers John Finch and Bob Grossman, with leaderships from Biggs Cunningham, competed at the Le Man race and established Corvette as a serious race competitor. The car beat out the famed racing cars of Jaguar, Ferrari, and Porsche!

- When No.9, a newly created V-8 Corvette, debuted at the 1967 24 Hours of Le Mans race with co-driver Dick Guldstrand and Bob Bondurant, it marked Corvette being seen as a true professional race car. The car hit speeds of 170 mph and was able to keep up with other racing cars. Unfortunately, due to a broken wrist pin, the car had to end the race early.

- In 2005, Corvette introduced the C6 R. With the V8 engine, it became more dependable and much faster. In 2006, Corvette won the class victory at 24 Hours at Le Mans.

- In 1988, a VH1 contest was held to win 36 Corvettes, one for each year of production between 1954 to 1989. The winner, Dennis Amodeo, would sell his collection to pop artist Peter Max, who planned on using them for art. Max would never use the Corvettes and they sat in a New York City parking garage until they were resold in 2012.

- A documentary series was created for the History Channel in 2019, showing the restoration of these Corvettes after nearly 20 years of sitting with popped tires and layers of dirt.

- The 1956 Cascade Green Corvette in the collection was used by Jerry Seinfeld for his show *Comedians in Cars Getting Coffee*. Seinfeld would drive around with comedian Jimmy Fallon.

- Jerry Seinfeld drove a 1963 Corvette Stingray with President Obama on his show *Comedians in Cars Getting Coffee*. The Stingray has a 5.4-liter V8 engine and the infamous split back rear window.

- Corvettes have been featured in hundreds of movies, yet not one of those movies was featured in an Academy Award or Golden Globe award.

- Drivers Bob Johnson and Dave Heinz drove an old "scrappy" Corvette at the 12 hours of Sebring race, and surprisingly placed 4th overall and won their 2.5-liter GT class victory in 1973.

- John Powell ran a racing school at Canada's Mosport track, following the ban of Corvettes at SCCA racing. Powell created this race for Corvette drivers, with a million-dollar prize. Fifty-six identical Corvettes were created for the competition.

CHAPTER 8:
FAMOUS USES OF CORVETTES IN MEDIA

TRIVIA TIME!

1. True or False: Corvettes were a symbol of freedom and adventure throughout the 1960s.

2. What 1978 movie starring Mark Hamill used Corvette in its title?

    a. *Corvette Dream*
    b. *Corvette Fever*
    c. *Corvette Summer*
    d. *Corvette Mile*

3. True or False: A Corvette has been used more times as the pace car at the Indianapolis 500 than any other car.

4. What color was the 1979 Corvette Indy 500 pace car painted?

    a. Black and silver
    b. Yellow and black
    c. White and red
    d. Silver and blue

5. The artist Prince wrote what song after a Corvette?
   a. "The Blue Corvette"
   b. "Little Red Corvette"
   c. "Little Corvette"
   d. "Corvette in Paradise"

6. True or False: A TV show aired in the 1980s called "Route 81" that featured a Corvette.

7. Cherry Valence from *The Outsiders* drove this color Corvette:
   a. Black
   b. White
   c. Blue
   d. Red

8. How many Grand Sport Corvettes were made in 1962?
   a. Three
   b. Five
   c. Seven
   d. Nine

9. True or False: Zora Arkus-Duntov saved the five Grand Sport cars from destruction.

10. With changes in materials for the 1962 Grand Sport, how much weight was taken off?
    a. 500 pounds
    b. 1,000 pounds
    c. 1,500 pounds
    d. 2,000 pounds

11. True or False: A 1966 Corvette C2 Sting Ray was driven by Letty Ortiz the in *The Fate of the Furious*.

12. This N.A.R.T. No. 4 Corvette was given the nickname "Old Scrappy" and raced against Ferrari Daytona and Porsche 911s.
    a. 1972 Corvette
    b. 1973 Corvette
    c. 1975 Corvette
    d. 1978 Corvette

13. N.A.R.T. No. 4 Corvette raced in which two international races?
    a. 24 hours of Le Mans and Watkins Glen Race
    b. 12 hours of Sebring and 24 Hours of Le Mans
    c. Monaco Grand Prix and 12 Hours of Sebring
    d. Nürburgring 24 Hours and 24 Hours of Le Mans

14. True or False: Corvette is the official sports car of Kentucky.

15. Driver Delmo Johnson drove what rare Corvette at his last international race in March 1965?
    a. 1964 Sting Ray
    b. 1962 Grand Sport
    c. 1969 ZL-1
    d. 1967 427

16. True or False: The musician Prince woke up in a Corvette and wrote a song "Little Red Corvette."

17. This 1988 Corvette was named "Cinemotion" and used for filming car movies. What featured did the car *not* have?
    a. Computer chip upgrade
    b. High flow exhaust
    c. Modified disc brakes
    d. Changed steering wheel

18. In the 1997 movie *Con Air*, DEA Agent Duncan Malloy drove what year Corvette?
    a. 1957 Corvette
    b. 1960 Corvette
    c. 1967 Corvette
    d. 1970 Corvette

19. What year was the first time a Corvette appeared in a film?

   a. 1955
   b. 1957
   c. 1959
   d. 1961

20. True or False: Patriotism helped sell Corvettes to returning World War II veterans.

21. This 2020 hit by Poppa Hunna ft. Lil Uzi Vert has reference to a Corvette. What is the name of the song?

   a. "Give Me More Power"
   b. "Race Car – Vroom"
   c. "Adderall (Corvette Corvette)"
   d. "Corvette Dreaming with You"

22. True or False: A Corvette Stingray was featured in *How It's Made: Dream Cars,* aired in 2014.

ANSWERS

1. True

2. C – Corvette Summer

3. True – It's been used 13 times.

4. A – Black and silver

5. B – "Little Red Corvette"

6. False – The show "Route 66" aired from 1960-1964 and featured a Corvette.

7. D – Red

8. B – Five

9. True

10. B – 1,000 pounds

11. True

12. A – 1972

13. B - 12 Hours of Sebring and 24 Hours of Le Mans

14. True

15. B – 1962 Grand Sport

16. False – He originally woke up in a Mercury and changed it to Corvette.

17. D – Changed steering wheel

18. C – 1967

19. A - 1955

20. True

21. C – "Adderall (Corvette Corvette)"

22. True

DID YOU KNOW?

- The 1979 Corvette Indy 500 pace car was painted black and silver in order to photograph better, given that newspapers printed in black and white.

- In 1960, the television show *Route 66* aired, and it featured two people driving a Corvette across the United States. During the four years the show aired, Chevrolet supplied a new Corvette with each season.

- The show *Route 66* was filmed in black and white, which led to fans believing that the Corvette was red, which added to the idea that "All Corvettes Are Red." The Corvette was actually a neutral metallic color of either Sateen Silver, Fawn Beige, and Saddle Tan. This was done because the neutral colors looked best on black and white film.

- The Beach Boys and Jan & Dean wrote songs that had Corvettes in them, which helped bring attention and demand to the vehicle. A Corvette would become the dream car for Baby Boomers that grew up in the 1960s and 1970s when Corvettes were the "it" car.

- In 1962, Zora Arkus-Duntov wanted to create winning race Corvettes. His project "Light Weight" called for 125 Grand Sport Corvettes to be produced. Five cars were created before GM canceled the project. The five models had body modifications, special suspensions, and new engines that reached 550 horsepower.

- With the 1962 Grand Sport, the idea was to create a lighter car that would be faster; the designers and engineers were able to do this. Using aluminum, magnesium, and ultra-thin fiberglass, the car was nearly 1,000 pounds lighter.

- Zora Arkus-Duntov saved the five 1962 Grand Sport Corvettes from destruction, saved two for himself, and gave three of them away.

- Famed driver Delmo Johnson would drive one of the five remaining Grand Sports. He drove #003 at his last international race at Sebring in March 1965.

- In 1972, a Corvette was purchased for $600. This car was used to race at Le Mans under the GT class, one of the top classes. It was given the nickname "Old Scrappy" due to repairing and rebuilding it each time it raced. When the GT class required a set amount of factory parts it was given the name N.A.R.T. No. 4 and even looked like a Ferrari.

- Prince famously wrote "Little Red Corvette" in 1982. Prince woke up in the back of his bandmate's 1964 pink Mercury Montclair Marauder. When he started writing the song, Corvette sounded better, and it stuck! "Little Red Corvette" was used in Chevrolet commercials with the tagline of "They Don't Write Songs About Volvos."

- Called "Hollywood's unsung racing hero," this adapted 1988 Corvette was used to film stunts and car scenes in movies. Also called "Cinemotion" a camera was attached to the front of the car and was able to match supercar speeds while also being able to break quickly. Powell Motor Sports added the upgrades: upgraded intakes, a computer chip upgrade, high flow exhaust, modified disc brakes, and increased torque band.

- The first Corvette generation C1 was marketed towards World War II veterans, while the C2 generation was marketed more as a sports car for "midlife" crises. These veterans wanted to buy American made vehicles, not German or Japanese cars.

- A Corvette C2 Sting Ray was used in the film *The Fate of the Furious*.

CHAPTER 9:
COLLECTIONS

TRIVIA TIME!

1. Where is the National Corvette Museum located?
    a. New York, New York
    b. St. Louis, Missouri
    c. Bowling Green, Kentucky
    d. Flint, Michigan

2. True or False: There were multiple 1983 Corvette models created.

3. How many of the 1983 models were destroyed?
    a. 0
    b. 9
    c. 39
    d. 59

4. What year Corvette is considered the most sought after by collectors?
    a. 1956
    b. 1959
    c. 1961
    d. 1963

5. True or False: The C2 String Ray is one of the most popular generations of Corvettes.

6. How many models of the 1969 ZL-1 427 model were made?

   a. One
   b. Two
   c. Three
   d. Four

7. True or False: This 2014 Corvette Stingray Convertible was sold for $1 million and donated to charity!

8. How much did the third ever produced 1953 Corvette sell for in 2006?

   a. $1.06 million
   b. $2.06 million
   c. $3.06 million
   d. $4.06 million

9. True or False: The 1963 to 1967 Sting Ray is one of the Top 100 Coolest cars according to *Automobile Magazine*.

10. How much did the ultra-rare 1963 Split Rear Window originally sell for?

    a. $3,500
    b. $4,500
    c. $5,500
    d. $6,500

11. How many of the ultra-rare 1963 were made?
    a. 278
    b. 578
    c. 778
    d. 978

12. How many model Corvettes does the largest *model collection* have?
    a. 1,500
    b. 1,700
    c. 1,900
    d. 2,100

13. How much was Briggs Cunningham's No. 1 Corvette driven at the 1960 Le Mans being sold for at auction?
    a. $1 million
    b. $1.5 million
    c. $2 million
    d. $2.5 million

14. True or False: The No. 1 Corvette raced at 1960 Le Mans was missing until 2000.

15. Bob McDorman has one of the best Corvette Collections. How many Corvettes were in his collection?
    a. 106
    b. 156
    c. 206
    d. 256

16. How many hours were spent restoring a 1953 Corvette following it being re-discovered in 2012?

   a. 2,000 hours
   b. 3,000 hours
   c. 4,000 hours
   d. 5,000 hours

17. How many miles did a rare 1965 Convertible Corvette have when it was discovered in 2020?

   a. 47,000 miles
   b. 57,000 miles
   c. 67,000 miles
   d. 77,000 miles

18. How many Corvette L89s in 1967 were created?

   a. 10
   b. 16
   c. 24
   d. 37

19. What year was the 100th anniversary of the founding of Chevrolet, which included a Centennial Edition of Corvettes that came out that year?

   a. 2002
   b. 2009
   c. 2012
   d. 2015

20. True or False: The Corvette Museum in Bowling Green, Kentucky is receiving a 30,000-square-foot expansion!

ANSWERS

1. C – Bowling Green, Kentucky
2. False – Only one was created.
3. D – 59 destroyed
4. D – 1963
5. True
6. B – Two
7. True – It was the first produced 2014 Corvette in 2013.
8. A – $1.06 million
9. True
10. C – $5,500
11. A – 278
12. B – 1,700
13. A – $1 million
14. False – It was not found until 2012.
15. D – 206
16. C – 4,000 hours
17. A – 47,000 miles
18. B – 16

19. C – 2012
20. True

DID YOU KNOW?

- The National Corvette Museum was created in 1994 and is located less than half a mile from the GM production factory in Bowling Green, Kentucky!

- Only one 1983 model Corvette is known to have existed. It is on display at the National Corvette Museum. Due to quality issues, GM stopped production of Corvettes in 1983, making this car one of the rarest Corvettes. Sixty of the cars were produced, but only one was kept the other 59 were destroyed.

- Many collectors consider the 1963 Grand Sport as one of the most sought-after Corvettes. Only five Grand Sports were produced for the racing program before it was shut down. It's estimated that if one of these cars were to go to auction it would go for an estimated $6 billion to $8 million.

- The 1963 String Ray is one of the most sought after ultra-rare Corvettes; these are the only models with split rear windows. Only 278 were produced and many people got rid of the rear window which added to the rarity!

- The 1963 String Ray also was the first Corvette with factory installed air conditioning. The AC was priced at $421, which made it the third most expensive option on the '63 Corvette order sheet. The cars with

AC had a factory decal that helps with the rare demand. A recent sale of this rare car sold for $205,000 with the original factory installed AC.

- In 2013, the first produced 2014 Corvette was auctioned for a charity and was purchased for $1 million dollars!
- With 47% of Corvette owners having a college degree, these drivers are some of the most educated car drivers. This is also higher than the national average.
- The largest collection of model Corvettes is a private collection in Oconomowoc, Wisconsin. There are 1,700 models and they are worth over $50,000.
- Three Corvettes were entered at the 1960 Le Mans race: No. 1, No. 2, No. 3, with the first of the Corvettes being the most famous even though it only raced 32 laps. No. 1 was driven by Briggs Cunningham and was discovered in a storage until in St. Petersburg, Florida in 2012. The car is going for auction in the fall of 2021, with an estimated $1 million price tag.
- When the "Lost 36" Corvettes were discovered in 2012 it took over 4,000 hours to fully restore the 1953 Corvette, while the 1989 Corvette only took 40 hours.
- In 2020, a rare 1965 "Fuelie" convertible Corvette was discovered in a garage under a pile of trash! The car was believed to have been parked in the 1960s

and left untouched. The car had 47,000 miles total, and extremely rare low milage.

- The car has a matching fuel injection with four speeds, and a 5.4 L, 327-inch V8 engine. Only 771 units were produced with this sized engine, which added to the rarity of this discovered car.

- The 1969 ZL-1 is considered an ultra-rare Corvette. The car was sold for $10,771 whereas the 2014 ZL-1 was sold for $78,996. This car was designed by Zora Arkus-Duntov and to be the ultimate "racer kit".

- In 1991 a Corvette ZL-1 was sold for $300,000 at auction by Roger Judski, the owner of the Corvette Center in Maitland, Florida.

CHAPTER 10:
THE FOUNDERS

TRIVIA TIME!

1. True or False: Louis Chevrolet, the co-founder of Chevrolet, was a race car driver.

2. What year was Chevrolet founded?
   a. 1905
   b. 1907
   c. 1909
   d. 1911

3. Louis Chevrolet invented this important piece of race cars.
   a. Circle Bar
   b. Roll Bar
   c. Flip Bar
   d. Side Bar

4. True or False: Did designer Harley Earl get inspiration from Jaguar cars, when designing the first Corvettes?

5. Who was called the "Father of the Corvette?"
   a. Zora Arkus–Duntov
   b. Harley Earl
   c. Thomas Keating
   d. Bob McLean

6. True or False: Designer Harley Earl and Chevrolet General Manager Thomas Keating considered creating different types of Corvettes.

7. What year did Harley Earl first create Corvette?
   a. 1950
   b. 1951
   c. 1952
   d. 1953

8. What was the secret code for the development of Corvettes?
   a. Ruby
   b. Opel
   c. Diamond
   d. Emerald

9. True or False: Harley Earl would attend road-racing events to get inspiration for Corvettes.

10. In what city did GM founder William Durant get inspiration behind the bowtie logo?

    a. London
    b. Detroit
    c. Paris
    d. New York City

11. True or False: It was designer Harley Earl that designed the general layout of the Corvette.

12. What was the first Corvette generation not designed by Zora Arkus–Duntov, following his 1975 retirement?

    a. C3
    b. C4
    c. C2
    d. C6

13. How many large-scale Corvette organizations are there nationwide?

    a. 3 groups
    b. 4 groups
    c. 5 groups
    d. 6 groups

14. True or False: Chevrolet struggled to sell Corvette when first produced, after poor production and lack of customer interest?

15. What year did Harley Earl retire?
    a. 1955
    b. 1957
    c. 1959
    d. 1961

16. Who convinced Chevrolet to install V8 engines to improve power and speed?
    a. Harley Earl
    b. Thomas Keating
    c. Bob McLean
    d. Zora Arkus-Duntov

17. True or False: Chevrolet sales in the early 1950s were an all-time high.

18. Between what years was David McLellan the chief engineer at Corvette?
    a. 1969-1983
    b. 1975-1992
    c. 1977- 1989
    d. 1980 -1995

19. True or False: Harley Earl was inspired to create a fiberglass body after seeing how Glasspar boat company created the Glasspar G2.

20. What was the "The Hammer Room?"
    a. Corvette Bathroom
    b. Corvette Development Room
    c. Corvette Engineers' Room
    d. Corvette Steel Shop

21. True or False: GM executive Jim Perkins left GM and four years later returned to the company?

22. Who designed the C2 Sting Ray Corvette?
    a. Bill Mitchell
    b. Zora Arkus-Duntov
    c. Harley Earl
    d. Bob McLean

ANSWERS

1. True

2. D – 1911

3. B – Roll Bar

4. True – He took inspiration for the Jaguar XK 120!

5. A – Zora Arkus–Duntov

6. True – They considered creating sister cars!

7. B – 1951

8. B – Opel

9. True

10. C – Paris

11. False – Bob Mclean designed the layout.

12. B – C4

13. A – 3 groups

14. True

15. C – 1959

16. D – Zora Arkus- Duntov

17. False

18. B – 1975 to 1992

19. True

20. C – Corvette Engineers' Room

21. True

22. A – Bill Mitchell

DID YOU KNOW?

- In 1911, race car drivers Louis Chevrolet and financier William Durant founded Chevrolet. Louis Chevrolet would invent the roll bar, which is now mandatory in all race cars! He left his mark on the racing world.

- When GM founder William Durant saw a wallpaper pattern in a Paris hotel in 1908, he loved it. It's rumored that Durant ripped part of the wallpaper off and brought it back with him to Detroit.

- Chevrolet General Manager Thomas Keating wanted to recover from declining Chevrolet sales. Keating decided to create an American-made sports car that would compete with the European cars of Jaguars and Ferraris. He wanted a price more reasonable, that allowed for an "average" person to be able to purchase the car.

- Designer Harley Earl is cited with designing Corvettes. One of his first designs, "Projects Opel," was created and fit under the price limit at $2,000. Earl and his group of "Special Projects" crew started the design of the Corvette in 1951!

- It was rumored that Harley Earl was too tall to fit properly in a Corvette; no photos of him were taken with him inside!

- When Bob McLean was designing the general layout of the Corvette, he was given the code name of "Opel" when talking about the car. At one point, the name "Opel" was considered for the new car.

- Sister Corvettes were considered by Harley Earl and Thomas Keating. These cars would be called the Motorama Nomad and *Crovair*.

- Belgium engineer Zora Arkus-Duntov, "The Father of Corvettes," joined the Corvette program after seeing the Motorama display in New York City in 1953! He would become the Chevrolet engineer. With Arkus-Duntov's innovative ideas he helped Corvette create true race cars with improved speed! Arkus-Duntov was given this prestigious title by the Automotive Hall of Fame.

- Zora Arkus-Duntov was one of the first engineers that had experience in race cars and driving high performance sports cars. Arkus-Duntov had driven for Allard and Porsche at the 24 hours at Le Mans race.

- Harley Earl was inspired by European sports cars, and would attend road-racing shows, such as the Watkins Glen races. He used these races to see how the cars preformed and looked!

- Harley Earl would retire only six years into creating Corvettes, in 1959. His career started in the 1920s when he began designing for GM and designed the Cadillac LaSalle.

- There are three main Corvette organizations in the United States: the National Corvette Restorers Society, the National Council of Corvette Clubs, and the C5/C6 Registry.

- Chevrolet struggled to sell Corvettes. Those wanting a fast car would buy European Ferraris or Jaguars. It was not until the change in engine to a V8 did Corvettes earn the respect from car enthusiasts. The market was not used to American-made sports cars. Following the use of V8 engines, Corvettes were entered into the racing community and started to beat European racing cars in races!

- In 1952, Harley Earl went to Costa Mesa, California. It was here that Earl saw how Glasspar boats used fiberglass. Earl shared the information with GM, and they made the choice to start manufacturing the Corvette's body.

- With the ban of racing, Zora Arkus-Duntov had to create a loophole in order to create a faster vehicle. Working with Roger Penske to create a better engine, to get the project approved they would classify it as an off-road use only, thus the Corvette L88 was created.

- In 1957, when Bill Mitchell returned from an auto show in Italy, he wanted to create another sports car.

Mitchell created a design team in the "Hammer Room," hidden behind an actual tool room at GM–this is the founding of the Stingray.

- It was rumored that Bill Mitchell had a shark mounted on his office wall!
- Jim Perkins started with Chevrolet in 1960 sorting parts in the warehouse. He would work his way up and become Assistant General Sales Manager. In 1984, Perkins left Chevrolet to join Toyota, and shockingly left the company four years later to return to GM! He even drove three of the Indy 500 pace cars!

CHAPTER 11:
CORVETTE RACING HISTORY

TRIVIA TIME!

1. What year marked Corvette's first professional race?
   a. 1955
   b. 1956
   c. 1957
   d. 1958

2. True or False: Corvette has the world's longest-running continuously produced passenger car.

3. How many Corvettes were entered in the 24 Hours of Le Mans race in 1960?
   a. 1 Corvette
   b. 2 Corvettes
   c. 3 Corvettes
   d. 4 Corvettes

4. In what year did Corvette win its first-class victory at 24 Hours of Le Mans race?

   a. 1959
   b. 1960
   c. 1961
   d. 1962

5. How many races has Corvette Racing won since 1999?

   a. 57
   b. 77
   c. 97
   d. 107

6. True or False: The 1960 Cunningham Corvette won the overall Le Mans race.

7. In what year did the V-8 Corvette debut at the 24 hours Le Mans?

   a. 1963
   b. 1965
   c. 1967
   d. 1970

8. True or False: The 2005 Corvette debuted the C6 R and would race until 2015.

9. How fast did the 1967 V-8 Corvette reach in the Le Mans race?

   a. 150 mph
   b. 155 mph
   c. 170 mph
   d. 175 mph

10. What feature did the 2017 Corvette C7.R and Z06 not have?

    a. Fiberglass Frame
    b. Engine Technology
    c. Aerodynamic Straggles
    d. Tire Construction

11. True or False: Only five 1963 Grand Sport Corvettes were created before the program was dropped.

12. How many miles has Corvette raced at Le Mans since 2000?

    a. 95,221,250 miles
    b. 105,221,250 miles
    c. 115,221,250 miles
    d. 125,221,250 miles

13. True or False: Chevrolet had officially agreed to be a part of an industry-wide ban on racing.

14. How many identical Corvettes were produced for the 1988 "Corvette Challenge?"

    a. 36
    b. 46
    c. 56
    d. 66

15. How much did the Corvette Challenge car cost to purchase?

    a. $23,043
    b. $26,043
    c. $33,043
    d. $36,043

16. Why was the 1988 Corvette Challenge created?

    a. Corvette had gotten in trouble for cheating.
    b. Corvette was banned from SCCA racing.
    c. Corvette drivers wanted to race each other.
    d. There was a lack of Corvette race wins.

17. In international racing, what does GT stand for? Example: GT Class at Le Mans race.

    a. Good Tour
    b. Golden Tow
    c. Great Team
    d. Grand Touring

18. True or False: Corvette Racing partnered with Pratt & Miller Engineering to create the race worthy Corvettes.

19. What year was the first Corvette NASCAR vehicle make?

   a. 1953
   b. 1957
   c. 1960
   d. 1963

20. When was the first time that Corvette served as the NASCAR pace car?

   a. 1958
   b. 1968
   c. 1978
   d. 1988

21. True or False: The 1966 Corvette was not eligible for the SCAA Trans Am race.

22. What racing class does Corvette Racing in?

   a. GTLM class
   b. LMP3 class
   c. DPi class
   d. GTD class

23. How many gallons of gas does the 2012 Corvette C6.R race car carry?

   a. 20.77 gallons
   b. 21.77 gallons
   c. 22.77 gallons
   d. 23.77 gallons

ANSWERS

1. B – 1956
2. True
3. C – 3 Corvettes
4. B – 1960
5. D – 107 wins
6. False – It won the class race and 8th overall.
7. C – 1967
8. False – Race until 2013
9. C – 170 mph
10. A – It had an aluminum frame.
11. True
12. A – 95,221,250 miles
13. True
14. C – 56 Corvettes
15. C – $33,043
16. B – Corvette was banned from SCCA races.
17. D – Grand Touring
18. True

19. A - 1953

20. C – 1978

21. True

22. A – GTLM

23. D – 23.77 gallons

DID YOU KNOW?

- In 1956, with the support from Chevrolet engineer Zora Arkus-Duntov, Corvette entered into its first professional race. The 12 Hours of Sebring race with five Corvettes marked the beginning of Corvette's racing history.

- When three Corvettes were entered for the 24 Hours of Le Mans race in 1960, this marked the vehicle's transition into an international racing car.

- During the 1960 24 Hours at Le Mans, the iconic No. 3 Corvette driven by John Fitch and Bob Grossman won their class and placed 8th overall in the race. Nineteen hours into the 24 Hours race, the engine started to overheat, and ice was packed into the engine to cool it down. It worked and No. 3 finished the race, marking the start of Corvette's history.

- Drivers Dick Guldstrand and Bob Bondurant were proving Corvette could compete with other vehicles at the 1967 Le Mans race. The car was able to reach speeds of 170 mph on the Mulsanna straight of the race. Their speed put them as front runners to win their class. A broken wrist pin would end the race for Corvette.

- Following the 1955 race accident in which a Mercedes 300 SLR exploded, killing 83 people, Chevrolet and many other American car companies agreed to ban racing. This was in part because they worried Congress would get involved.

- In 1999, when Corvette Racing was established, it marked a new age of modern Corvette racing. Since 1999, the program has won 107 victories, more than any other program in the International Motor Sports Association. Including eight wins at Le Mans, three wins at Rolex 24 at Daytona, and 11 wins at the Mobil 1 Twelve Hours of Sebring.

- In 1963, five Grand Sport Corvettes were created before the program was dumped. Chevrolet engineer Zora Arkus-Duntov created the cars to have a tube frame, with wide wheels with new suspension, and an all-aluminum 337-cubic-inch V-8 engine that had 550 horsepower.

- Corvettes were winning many of the SCCA (Sport Car Club of America) races throughout the 1980s, which resulted in the club banning Corvettes from racing. Companies of Porsche and Lotus were upset with Corvette's winning streak. With the ban, John Powell suggested and created the Corvette Challenge, a race with only Corvettes. The prize for winning would be one million dollars.

- Fifty-six identical Corvettes were created and purchased to ensure a fair race; no modifications were allowed. The only difference in the cars was their color. These 1988 Corvettes had high horsepower V8 engines, aerodynamic bodies, and rigid suspensions. It was up to the driver to win the race, not any changes made to the car.

- In 1966, a Corvette was not eligible for the SCCA Trans Am race. This was because of the upper limit of the 5.0 liter on the engine. The only Chevrolet car that was eligible was the Corvair.

- Corvette Racing would race in the GTLM class, which is being replaced and will be the GTD Pro class!

- As of 2013, the Corvette Racing team is the most successful team in the history of American Le Mans series competition. As of 2013, they have had 54 one-two finishes and seven class victories at 24 Hours of Le Mans,

CHAPTER 12:
CORVETTE SPECS

TRIVIA TIME!

1. What was the most popular color for the 1967 Corvette?
   a. Rally Red
   b. Marina Blue
   c. Sunfire Yellow
   d. Goodwood Green

2. In 1967, how much did air conditioning cost to be in a Corvette?
   a. $412.90
   b. $512.90
   c. $612.90
   d. $712.90

3. How many convertible 1999 Corvettes were created?
   a. 8,161
   b. 10,161
   c. 11,161
   d. 15,161

4. True or False: Nassau Blue Metallic is one the rarest Corvette color.

5. How much did the base 1955 Corvette cost?
   a. $1,774
   b. $2,774
   c. $3,774
   d. $4,774

6. How much did the 1977 Model 19437 Sport Coupe weight?
   a. 3,543 lb.
   b. 5,543 lb.
   c. 7,543 lb.
   d. 9,543 lb.

7. What was the most popular exterior color in 2012?
   a. Cyber Grey
   b. Inferno Orange
   c. Torch Red
   d. Carlisle Blue

8. Why did the 1962 327 have a nickname of "Fuelie?"
   a. Optional Fuel Injection System
   b. Single Fuel Tank
   c. Twin Double Fuel Tank
   d. Large Fuel Tank

9. True or False: Astronaut Alan Bean received a one-of-a kind Corvette in 1969.

10. The 1963 Corvette Z06 is called "Big Tank." How many gallons did the gas tank hold?

   a. 24.5 gallons
   b. 26.5 gallons
   c. 34.5 gallons
   d. 36.5 gallons

11. How much did factory air conditioning cost in 1963?

   a. $421
   b. $467
   c. $493
   d. $512

12. True or False: Corvette replaced the glovebox in 1994.

13. How many 1976 Stingrays were produced with rear window defrost?

   a. 14,960
   b. 24,960
   c. 34,960
   d. 44,960

14. What Corvette made an impression in the racing world?

   a. C3-Z
   b. L88
   c. C2 5F0
   d. C5-R

15. How fast can the 2017 Corvette Grand Sport reach in 0-60 mph?

    a. 1.5 seconds
    b. 2.7 seconds
    c. 3.6 seconds
    d. 4.9 seconds

16. How many fin alloy valve covers did the 1956 Corvette have?

    a. Five
    b. Seven
    c. Nine
    d. Eleven

17. How many exterior colors were offered in 1982 and 1987?

    a. 8 colors
    b. 10 colors
    c. 14 colors
    d. 16 colors

18. In what year did the first Corvette have an 85 MPH speedometer?

    a. 1980
    b. 1982
    c. 1984
    d. 1986

19. How many manual transmissions does the 2014 Stingray have?

   a. Four
   b. Five
   c. Seven
   d. Eight

20. How much did a 350-cu. in. 210hp engine cost in the 1976 Corvette?

   a. $381.00
   b. $481.00
   c. $581.00
   d. $681.00

21. What is the 2021 Corvette Stingray coupe starting price?

   a. $59,900
   b. $69,900
   c. $79,900
   d. $89,900

22. How many Stingrays were made the first year, in 1963?

   a. 11,000
   b. 15,000
   c. 21,000
   d. 25,000

23. What was the first year that glass T-tops were offered?

    a. 1972
    b. 1974
    c. 1976
    d. 1978

24. What was the price for a Corvette in 1953?

    a. $1,490
    b. $2,490
    c. $3,490
    d. $4,490

ANSWERS

1. B – Marina Blue
2. A – $412.90
3. C – 11,161
4. True
5. B – $2,774
6. A – 3,534 lb.
7. C – Torch Red
8. A – Optional Fuel Injection System
9. True
10. D – 36.5 gallons
11. A – $421
12. True
13. B – 24,960
14. D – 1999 to 2004 C5-R
15. C – 3.6 seconds
16. C – Nine
17. D – 16 Colors
18. A – 1980

19. C – Seven

20. B - $481.00

21. A - $59,900

22. C – 21,000 Stingrays

23. D – 1978

24. C - $4,490

DID YOU KNOW?

- Nassau Blue Metallic is one of the rarest colors. The color stopped being offered in 2000, with only 851 units having this color. This is the only color that has been applied to under 1,000 Corvette units.

- In the early 1960s, having a vehicle that could reach 360 horsepower was rare, unless in a sedan. Corvette wanted a fast, smaller vehicle that was not the weight or size of a sedan!

- When Corvette introduced the option of a fuel injection system, the Corvette 327 was given the nickname "Fuelie." The car was also able to reach speeds of 110 mph!

- Alan Bean's rare Corvette is the only "Astrovette" remaining. Bean's Corvette was specially created with a four-speed wide-range transmission, 390-hp, and 427 Turbo-Jet V-8 engine. Bean's initials were even carved into the side of the car!

- Alan Bean and other astronauts would race their cars together, near the Kennedy International Space Station in Flordia!

- Earning the nickname "Big Tank," this 1963 Z06 Corvette has a 36.5-gallon tank along with a L84 engine. The gas tank was much larger than other models, resulting in the nickname!

- Only 50 of the "Big Tank" Corvettes were created. The engine could reach 360 hp and had large brakes that allowed the car to stop faster. This model is now a sought-after collector's item.

- In 1994, Corvette installed a passenger side airbag, resulting in the need to remove the glovebox. This removal was not favored among drivers, and pockets were added into the door panel to make up for the lack of storage.

- Between production years of 1982 to 1987, there were 16 exterior paint colors offered. Some of the most popular colors were Dark Red Metallic, Bright Red, and Black. While some of the least popular colors were Light Blue Metallic, Dark Bronze Metallic, and Gold Metallic!

- In 1999, the year of the Corvette Racing, a total of 33,270 Corvettes were produced, with 18,078 being coupes and 11,161 being convertibles.

- Only created for racing, and not available for general public sale, the 1999 to 2004 C5-R was created to win. The car had a lightweight fiberglass body and ground-effects; the car was race-ready! The fame of this car came primarily from its success at the 24 Hours of Le Mans race.

- Getting its name from the limited 1963 Grand Sport Corvettes, the 2017 Grand Sport can reach impressive speeds, reaching 0-60 mph in 3.6 seconds and having impressive breaking ability.

- In 1963, when the Stingray was first produced, 21,000 vehicles were produced– half being coupes and half convertibles.
- The 2021 Corvette Stingray coupe has a starting price of $59,900 with the convertible model having a starting price of $67,400!
- The price to purchase an original Corvette in 1953 was $3,490, or $33,758 in 2020 dollars!

CHAPTER 13:
RARE CORVETTES

TRIVIA TIME!

1. How many were painted with Inca Silver acrylic lacquer in 1957?

    a. 50
    b. 55
    c. 60
    d. 65

2. What year is the rarest Corvette?

    a. 1968
    b. 1969
    c. 1970
    d. 1971

3. True or False: Turquoise is the rarest Corvette color.

4. How many Corvettes were produced with a split window?

    a. 500
    b. 1,000
    c. 1,500
    d. 2,000

5. This ultra-rare red coupe is one of only 20 cars to have the L88 package in 1967. How much did this Corvette sell for in auction in 2014?

   a. $1.85 million
   b. $2.85 million
   c. $3.85 million
   d. $4.85 million

6. With the muscle car wars ending, how many 1971 Corvette Z52 were built?

   a. Twelve
   b. Fifteen
   c. Eighteen
   d. Twenty-four

7. How much did the ZL1 package cost for the 1969 ZL1 Corvette?

   a. $3,000
   b. $4,000
   c. $5,000
   d. $6,000

8. How much did a *Hot Wheels* Corvette Stingray Gray with Orange Stripe sell for at auction?

   a. $450
   b. $475
   c. $500
   d. $525

9. What is the most sought-after collectible Corvette?

   a. 1961 Stingray
   b. 1963 Stingray
   c. 1977 Stingray
   d. 1980 Stingray

10. Due to limitation from the industry competition ban, how much HP could the 1967-69 L88 provide?

    a. 335 HP
    b. 395 HP
    c. 435 HP
    d. 495 HP

11. How many 427-Limited Edition Z06 Corvettes were released in 2008?

    a. 405
    b. 505
    c. 605
    d. 705

12. What feature was not included in the limited edition 1996 Grand Sport convertible?

    a. 330 Horsepower
    b. LT4 engine
    c. Changed exhaust system
    d. 6,300 RPM Rev Limiter

13. How much did a 1969 L88 Corvette sell for at auction?

    a. $478,000
    b. $578,000
    c. $678,000
    d. $778,000

14. What race was the 1963 Grand Sport supposed to debut at before GM canceled the project?

    a. Daytona 24 Hours
    b. 24 Hours at Le Mans
    c. Sebring 24 Hour
    d. Indianapolis 500

15. True or False: A blue SR-2 Corvette was created for Harley Earl's son in 1956.

16. How much did the SR2 #1, owned by Jerry Earl, sell for at auction in 2015?

    a. $4,885,000
    b. $5,885,000
    c. $6,885,000
    d. $8,885,000

17. What year Corvette was created for racetracks, not street cars, and Corvette tried to discourage people from purchasing?

   a. 1965 L88
   b. 1967 L88
   c. 1969 L88
   d. 1971 L88

18. What rare color was used for the last Corvettes produced in 1998?

   a. Pink Opel Metallic
   b. Green Emerald Metallic
   c. Purple Pearl Metallic
   d. Blue Topaz Metallic

19. What year saw the Corvette Trivia Board game?

   a. 1980
   b. 1982
   c. 1983
   d. 1985

20. What is the only Corvette that saw a one-year-only body design?

   a. 1970
   b. 1971
   c. 1972
   d. 1973

21. What feature was not included in the 1970 LT-1 package?

    a. Fiberglass Steering Wheel
    b. Holley Carburetor
    c. Special big-block hood
    d. 2.5-inch exhaust

22. How much did the ultra-rare Genovation GXE Corvette C7 sell for?

    a. $740,000
    b. $745,000
    c. $750,000
    d. $755,000

ANSWERS

1. D - 65
2. B – 1969
3. True
4. B – 1,000 created
5. C - $3.85 million
6. A – Twelve
7. D - $6,000
8. B - $475
9. B – 1963
10. C – 435 HP
11. B – 505
12. C – Changed Exhaust System
13. A - $478,000
14. B – 24 Hours at Le Mans
15. True
16. C - $6,885,000
17. B – 1967 L88
18. C – Purple Pearl Metallic

19. D – 1985

20. D – 1973

21. A - Fiberglass Steering Wheel

22. C - $750,000

DID YOU KNOW?

- In 1959, only 217 turquoise Corvettes were created, making it one of the rarest colors!

- In 2014, a 1967 L88 Corvette sold for $3.85 million at auction. Only 20 cars with the L88 package were created that year. Another L88 Corvette-Sunfire Yellow coupe is also being auctioned for a reported $2.69 million. These ultra-rare Corvettes have been fully restored, with the only Duntov and Triple Diamond Corvettes with the original engine!

- Due to industry changes, with unleaded gas becoming the standard fuel, vehicles were adapting. The demand for a "muscle car" was low, resulting in only 12 ZR2s to be created– ten coupe, and two convertibles.

- The $6,000 additional price for the ZL1 package resulted in only two of these Corvettes to be made. The package also did not include air conditioning or a radio– the high price of the package is the primary reason that only two were made.

- Released in 1978 for a limited time, the Corvette Stingray with limited gray and orange colors is viewed as a collection item and even sold for $475 in auction, making it one of the most expensive Hot Wheels toys sold!

- The 1963 Stingray has become one of the most sought-after Corvettes because of its rear window.

This split-window was only produced for one year, and after nearly 60 years not many of the original windows remain– making it extremely rare.

- The industry-wide competition ban proved to be difficult for Corvette designers. Cars were limited on how much horsepower they could provide. The 1967-69 L88 Corvette pushed the boundaries and reaches an impressive 435HP, making it one of the fastest cars available at the time, with only 216 being produced.

- When Corvette Assembly Plant Manager Wil Cooksey retired in 2008, a limited edition Z06 was released in his honor. The 427-Limited Edition was painted in Crystal Red Metallic paint; each was hand signed by Cooksey.

- The 1963 Grand Sport, the "baby" design for Zora Arkus-Duntov, had 125 units produced. Corvette was hoping to debut this new race car at the Le Mans race, but never made it given GM would cancel the project with only five models made.

- One of the first race cars built by Corvette was for Jerry Earl, the son of GM's design chief Harley Earl. Jerry was a road racer and was racing against Ferrari and wanted a fast car. His car was a blue SR-2 that differed from the other 1956 models.

- A second SR-2 was built for designer Bill Mitchell, which he had painted red and made with a high-fin design. Mitchell would drive his one-of-a-kind vehicle on the street. Bill Michell would also create another Corvette for himself, a 1958 Corvette XP-700.

- The 1967 Corvette L88 was created to be used for track racing, and not for street use; the vehicle had 430 hp. Only 216 of these L88s were built between 1967 and 1969, with only 20 made in 1967!

- In 1998, Corvette released a limited-edition color of "Medium Purple Pearl Metallic," and 381 of these Corvettes were created.

- 1973 saw the only year that Corvette made a body design for only one year of production. This Corvette featured a rubber front bumper and a chrome rear bumper. This differed from the past years that saw chrome bumpers on the front and back!

- Genovation is a small car building company, and they are able to create fast electric cars, including Corvettes! The C7 Corvette is $750,000 with only 75 made– the car can reach speeds of over 200 mph!

CHAPTER 14:
CORVETTE PAINT COLORS

TRIVIA TIME!

1. What exterior color was not offered for the 1955 Corvette?
    a. Harvest Gold
    b. Corvette Copper
    c. Polo White
    d. Fire Red

2. What year saw the first paint color in acrylic lacquer rather than nitrocellulose lacquer?
    a. 1952
    b. 1953
    c. 1955
    d. 1957

3. What was the most popular color Corvette in 1959?
    a. Tuxedo Black
    b. Snowcrest White
    c. Crown Sapphire
    d. Roman Red

4. What year saw colors of Ermine White, Sateen Silver Metallic, and Fawn Beige Metallic?

a. 1961
   b. 1962
   c. 1963
   d. 1964

5. True or False: "Purple People Eater" was a color offered in 1964?

6. How many colors were offered in 1963?
   a. Four
   b. Six
   c. Eight
   d. Ten

7. How many metallic colors were offered in 1966 for the exterior?
   a. Two
   b. Four
   c. Six
   d. Eight

8. How many Classic White Corvettes were ordered between 1968 and 1982?
   a. 33,681
   b. 43,681
   c. 53,681
   d. 63,681

9. What was the most popular Corvette color in 1975?

   a. Bright Blue
   b. Orange Flame
   c. Mille Miglia Red
   d. Classic Yellow

10. Between what years was Mille Miglia Red offered?

    a. 1970 to 1980
    b. 1965 to 1972
    c. 1971 to 1975
    d. 1973 to 1979

11. What was the most popular color for the 1986 C4 Corvette production?

    a. Bright Red
    b. Dark Red Metallic
    c. Black
    d. Cooper Metallic

12. How many 1988 Corvettes were painted in White, the most popular color that year?

    a. 3,020
    b. 3,620
    c. 4,020
    d. 4,620

13. What year saw the top three most popular colors of Sebring Silver Metallic (25.13%), Torch Red (20.51%), and Black (18.19%)?

    a. 1995
    b. 1996
    c. 1997
    d. 1998

14. What was the most popular color for the C5 generation?

    a. Torch Red
    b. Millennium Yellow
    c. Black
    d. Navy Blue Metallic

15. True or False: Black would become the most popular color for the 6th generation Corvette.

16. How many Corvette generations was white exterior paint on hiatus for?

    a. One
    b. Two
    c. Three
    d. Four

17. What was the least popular color for the 2001 Corvette?

    a. Dark Bowling Green Metallic
    b. Torch Red
    c. Light Pewter Metallic
    d. Millennium Yellow

18. What was the most popular Corvette color in 2006?

    a. LeMans Blue
    b. Velocity Yellow
    c. Black
    d. Victory Red

19. What year saw the top three most popular colors of Arctic White (1), Watkins Glen Gray (2), and Black (3)?

    a. 2014
    b. 2015
    c. 2016
    d. 2017

20. What two colors are new for Corvette in 2021?

    a. Machine Silver and Velocity Yellow
    b. Red Mist Tintcoat Metallic and Silver Flare Metallic
    c. Atomic Orange and Jetstream Blue
    d. LeMans Blue and Sunset Orange Pearl

ANSWERS

1. A – Fire Red
2. D – 1957
3. B – Snowcrest White
4. A – 1961
5. False – It was offered in 1959!
6. C – Eight Colors
7. C – Six Metallic Colors
8. B – 43,681
9. D – Classic White
10. C – 1971 to 1975
11. A – Bright Red
12. B – 3,620
13. B – 1996
14. A – Torch Red
15. True
16. C – Three
17. A – Dark Bowling Green Metallic – with 919 (2.58%) made
18. C – Black – with 7,243 (21.29%) made

19. D - 2017

20. B - Red Mist Tint Coat Metallic and Silver Flare Metallic

DID YOU KNOW?

- In 1955, five colors were offered for the exterior of the vehicle: Polo White, Pennant Blue, Corvette Copper, Gypsy Red, and Harvest Gold.

- "Corvette Copper," offered in 1955, was renamed to "Aztec Copper" for the 1956 and 1957 production years. Many Corvette fans claim the two colors are different, but they have the same DuPont color code, making them the same!

- For the first few years of Corvette production, the vehicles were painted in nitrocellulose lacquer, until 1957 when the new Inca Silver Metallic paint was used in acrylic lacquer. Only 100 Corvettes were produced in that color, and 1958 saw 36 produced with black paint covers.

- The first metallic color was offered in 1957 and became a very popular shade among Corvette owners. Soon metallic colors were being offered in all shades, including silver, turquoise, charcoal, and frost blue!

- During the 1959 production year, the most popular was Snowcrest White with 34.68% of the production that year, followed by Tuxedo Black at 16.48% and Frost Blue at 10.59%.

- In 1959 Corvette released three "Purple People Eaters," MKIII Corvettes! This car was built by

Nickey Chevrolet in Chicago to race and earned its name from being painted purple. During this time the song "Flying Purple People Eater" by Sheb Wooley was a hit in June 1958!

- Mille Miglia Red was offered from 1971 to 1975. This bright red shade was named after the Italian countryside race that had ended in the 1950s. Mille Miglia means "Thousand Miles" in Italian.

- The 1988 Corvette C4 offered a 35th Anniversary Special Edition package– this package was nearly $5,000 extra. The car had an all-white exterior and interior with white wheels and white door handles!

- For the C4 and C5 generation, the exterior color of red became the new most popular color, beating out white that had dominated for the previous years.

- Between 2005 and 2013, the color black became the most popular color, with 46,508 black Corvettes produced that year. The second most popular shade is Victory Red with 32,817 in that color produced.

- For three Corvette generations the color white was not offered, but the seventh generations Corvette brought it back. It became a popular color and 35,936 vehicles in Arctic White were ordered between 2014 and 2019.

- To honor the year 2000, Corvette released a limited-edition color, which included Millennium Yellow!

- In 2001, the least popular color was Dark Bowling Green Metallic with only 919 Corvettes in this color, only 2.58%

- Torch Red, Arctic White, and Black are the three most popular Corvette colors, followed by Sebring Orange, Elkhart Lake Blue, and Rapid Blue. Torch Red accounts for 25% of Corvette colors!

CHAPTER 15:
RANDOM FACTS

TRIVIA TIME!

1. Why did the serial number for the first air conditioning and the Corvette have a six-month difference?
   a. The technology didn't exist when the Corvette was first released, and they decided to update the vehicle when the AC became available.
   b. The Corvette owner was a GM executive, and he had the car refitted for AC six months later.
   c. There was a production error and the Corvette was prematurely released before completion.
   d. The Corvette's original design did not include an AC, but the first owners to purchase were disappointed enough at not having it that GM decided to re-make the Corvette to include the AC.

2. In what year was the first computer installed in a Corvette?

   a. 1979
   b. 1981
   c. 1984
   d. 1987

3. Why did the 1963 roof panel mold not fit?

4. Why did the 1967 Corvette drive to the track at Le Mans instead of being towed?

5. True or False: 1997 Corvette windshield wipers sweep in the same direction.

6. What year was the first time AM/FM stereo offered?

   a. 1967
   b. 1968
   c. 1969
   d. 1970

7. Why were aluminum wheels unavailable from 1973 to 1976?

8. What color replaced the original Polo White?

   a. Owl White
   b. Bleach White
   c. Snowcrest White
   d. Cloud White

9. True or False: Myron Scott, who named the Corvette, also invented the Soap Box Derby Race.

10. Why did designer Bill Mitchell want the 1963 spilt rear window?

11. The 1970s infamous Chevrolet campaign featured all but what?
    a. Baseball
    b. Hot Dogs
    c. Apple Pie
    d. American Flag

12. What Corvette is often viewed as the "ugliest model?"
    a. 1979 Pace Car
    b. 1991 Pace Car
    c. 1998 Pace Car
    d. 2001 Pace Car

13. What does the "T" in T-Top stand for in the C3 generation?

14. How many 1986 Corvettes were sent to Lotus in England to be converted into ZR1 prototypes?
    a. 20
    b. 30
    c. 40
    d. 50

15. True or False: In the '96 Grand Sport, did the race stripe stay the same width across the entire car?

16. Which color *was not* a new color to celebrate 2000 and Y2K Corvette edition?

   a. Millennium Yellow
   b. St. Louis Blue
   c. Dark Bowling Green Metallic

17. As of September 2020, how many Corvettes have been produced?

   a. 1 million
   b. 1.50 million
   c. 1.75 million
   d. 2 million

18. How many "Copper Metallic" Corvettes were created in 1986?

   a. 4
   b. 104
   c. 204
   d. 304

19. How much did the custom Corvette from the film *Corvette Summer* sell for?

   a. $25,000
   b. $30,000
   c. $35,000
   d. $40,000

20. How many of the first produced Corvettes were destroyed during testing?

   a. One
   b. Two
   c. Three
   d. Four

21. Across the early 1950s, how many European Sports Cars were imported to the United States?

   a. 10,000
   b. 15,000
   c. 20,000
   d. 25,000

22. How many of the 1983 pilot cars were created, before they were destroyed?

   a. 43 Corvettes
   b. 53 Corvettes
   c. 63 Corvettes
   d. 73 Corvettes

ANSWERS

1. B – The Corvette owner was a GM executive, and he had the car refitted for AC six months later.

2. B – 1981

3. The wrong side of the dimensions were used, resulting in the panels being too small.

4. The trailer that would have brought the Corvette to the track was full of car parts, thus no room to fit the Corvette.

5. True

6. B – 1968

7. The wheels were unable to hold air. The same issues arose in 1963 when aluminum wheels were first introduced.

8. C – Snowcrest White

9. True

10. Mitchell felt that the split window offered a more elegant and better aesthetic look, and that this new idea would help Corvette seem classy.

11. D – American flag was not included

12. C – 1998 Pace Car

13. The "T" stands for Targa Top. The original design

wanted all Targa, but a center bar was later determined to be needed.

14. A –20

15. False – The stripe gets wider up the hood, and narrower over the roof, and again wider in the back of the car.

16. B – St. Louis Blue

17. C – 1.75 million

18. A – 4 created

19. B - $30,000

20. B – Two were destroyed .

21. C – 20,000

22. A – 43 Corvettes

DID YOU KNOW?

- The roof panel gap was seen in the door pillar above the door on some of the models between 1963 and 1967. Any gaps were filled in and repaired with body filler.

- Prior to 1997, windshield wipers would sweep in opposite directions. Following 1997, the wipers swept in the same direction.

- In 1958, the original Polo White was replaced with Snowcrest White. Other colors added that year were Regal Turquoise, Signet Red, Panama Yellow, and silver.

- Corvette Designer Bill Mitchell felt that the split window offered a more elegant and better aesthetic look, and that this new idea would help Corvette seem classy.

- Myron Scott was the Chief of Photography at Chevrolet; it was Scott that suggested the name Corvette! Scott is also known for his pioneering of the Soap Box Derby race.

- In 1975, the commercial aid for Chevrolet featured this slogan: "Baseball, Hot Dogs, Apple Pie, and Chevrolet." Ed Labunski created the jingle for the commercial, and this slogan became one of the most recognized slogans in commercial history.

- The 1998 pace car for the Indianapolis 500 has been viewed as one of the "ugliest" Corvettes ever created. The car gained attention from the overuse of yellow, including yellow upholstery and rims!

- In 1986, Corvette sent twenty new vehicles to Lotus in England. This would start the long relationship between the two companies. The LT5 powered protypes were used for the ZR1 project; Corvette wanted to create faster cars.

- To celebrate the year 2000, Corvette released a limited edition C5 Corvette that featured two new colors Millennium Yellow and Dark Bowling Green Metallic.

- Only four Corvettes were ever produced with "Copper Metallic" color. One of the main reasons for the limited release was that producing the color was difficult. The reason for limited color was due to GM concerns over the quality! Only 87 "Copper Metallic" Corvettes were produced the year after in 1987.

- The first two Corvettes off the assembly line in 1953 were destroyed during testing. Chevrolet sent the third Corvette to Lockport, New York, for a cold weather test with expectations that the fiberglass body could handle the sub-freezing temperatures.

- One of these tests was called the "Shake Test." With 14 hours of dynamometer driving the wheels, each of the wheels had a weight to place to phase it, and all this was done at 20 degrees Fahrenheit. The #003 Corvette passed the tests, where it was sent back to Michigan and began 5,000 miles of testing on the Belgian block road.

- The #003 Corvette that survived the testing would be sold at auction in 2006 for $1.1 million.
- In 1983, Corvette had issues with production and did not release a model that year that had created 43 pilot cars. All but one of these cars were destroyed and the sole survivor is now on display at the Corvette Museum.

CHAPTER 16:
CORVETTES, CRIMES, AND ACCIDENTS

TRIVIA TIME!

1. What year Corvette is most likely to be stolen, according to NICB?
    a. 1980
    b. 1982
    c. 1984
    d. 1986

2. True or False: Corvettes have a fatal accident rate of 9.8 cars per billion miles.

3. What year were "safety cushions," later known as air bags, invented?
    a. 1952
    b. 1953
    c. 1954
    d. 1955

4. How many Corvettes were stolen in the largest Corvette heist in history?

    a. 5,554
    b. 6,554
    c. 7,554
    d. 8,554

5. What American serial killer was caught with a Corvette?

    a. Ted Bundy
    b. Jeffery Dahmer
    c. Robert Yates Lee Jr.
    d. John Wayne Gacy

6. What color Corvette was the above serial killer driving?

    a. White
    b. Red
    c. Blue
    d. Black

7. What state saw the most Corvette stealing between 1981 and 2011?

    a. California
    b. New York
    c. New Jersey
    d. Texas

8. True or False: VINs weren't required until 1981, making it difficult to track stolen cars.

9. What color car tends to be pulled over more by police?

   a. Red
   b. White
   c. Grey
   d. Silver

10. What code does the motor industry use when referring to stolen and recovered vehicles?

    a. Code 1
    b. Code 2
    c. Code 3
    d. Code 4

11. What percentage of Corvettes have been stolen since 1953?

    a. 5 percent
    b. 6 percent
    c. 7 percent
    d. 8 percent

12. The police TV show *Adam-12* featured what colored Corvette?

    a. Metallic Blue
    b. Metallic Red
    c. Metallic Yellow
    d. Metallic Green

13. True or False: Corvettes were voted one of the least accident-prone vehicles.

14. How many times has Corvette recalled a vehicle?
    a. 7 times
    b. 17 times
    c. 27 times
    d. 37 times

15. What year Corvette has been recalled the most times?
    a. 1995
    b. 1996
    c. 1997
    d. 1998

16. Between 2000 and 2014, what year had the most stolen models?
    a. 2001
    b. 2003
    c. 2005
    d. 2007

17. What safety feature was not included in the 2020 Corvette?
    a. Rear Cross Traffic Alert
    b. Advanced Theft Deterrent
    c. Slide Blind Zone Alert
    d. Self-Driving Safety Alert

18. True or False: The 1960 Corvette had recessed safety reflectors on the door sidewall panel?

19. What year had seat belts mandatory in vehicles per the Federal Motor Vehicle Safety Standard 208?

   a. 1981
   b. 1982
   c. 1983
   d. 1984

20. What was the first state to legally require seat belts in 1984?

   a. California
   b. New York
   c. Washington
   d. Massachusetts

ANSWERS

1. C – 1984
2. True
3. B – 1953
4. D – 8,554
5. C – Robert Yates Lee Jr.
6. A – White 1977 Corvette
7. A – California
8. True
9. B – White
10. C – Code 3
11. B – 6 percent
12. A – Metallic Blue
13. True
14. D – 37 times
15. C – 1997 Corvette
16. A – 2001
17. Self-Driving Safety Alert
18. True!
19. D – 1984
20. B – New York

DID YOU KNOW?

- The NICB (National Insurance Crime Bureau) reported that between 1981 and 2011, a 1984 Corvette was the most stolen Corvette, with 8,554 being reported. One of the reasons for this Corvette model being stolen the most is because of the high production– 1984 was the second most produced year of Corvettes in its history.

- The second most reported stolen car according to NICB, between 1981 and 2011, was the 1981 Corvette.

- 1992 to present, Corvettes have a high fatal accident rate, with 9.8 per billion million. This is the second-highest rate in recent vehicles. The reasoning behind this high statistic is that Corvette drivers tend to be wealthier people and drive more recklessly– leading to death.

- California saw the highest number of Corvette thieves between 1981 and 2011, with 14,002 reported, followed by Florida with 8,731 and Texas at 8,198.

- An industrial engineer's technician, John Hetrick, created and patented the first "safety cushion assembly for automotive vehicles" in 1953. He would contact Ford, GM, and Chrysler about this and never heard back. It was not until 1965 that air bags were concerned. It the 1970s, vehicles started to be equipped with them, and in 1991 laws were passed requiring air bags!

- American serial killer Robert Yates Lee drove a white 1977 Corvette, and this helped lead to his arrest. One of his victims remembered, survived, and was able to identify the vehicle.

- Robert Yates Lee brought unwanted attention to Corvette after he was arrested, and it was revealed that he learned to drive a white 1977 Corvette to find his victims. In 2005, the Corvette was placed for auction with limited bidders. A retired police officer would purchase the car for $4,000.

- With early Corvette thief records, it is difficult to find the stolen cars or know the accuracy of the data. This is because VIN (vehicle identification numbers) were not required until 1981.

- Against the popular urban myth, red color cars are the second must likely vehicle to be pulled over by police- the most common color is white!

- In the police T.V. show *Adam-12*, Officer Jim Reed drove a metallic blue Corvette. This car was the same make and model as the T.V. show *Route 66*.

- Corvette has recalled 37 vehicles, with seven of the recalls coming from the 1997 model.

- J.D. Power has rated Corvettes highly for reliability and recently gave the 2021 model a four out of five rating, which is higher than a lot of Corvettes competitors.

- Between 2000 and 2014, the most Corvettes were stolen was in 2001 with 124 reported thieves.
- Prior to 1968, seatbelts were not federally required in cars. This was until the Federal Motor Vehicle Safety Standard was passed in 1968. The first state to legally require seat belts was New York in 1984, due to John D. States, an orthopedic surgeon who wanted to improve vehicle safety measures.

CHAPTER 17:
WHAT IN THE WORLD?

TRIVIA TIME!

1. During what iconic Corvette year did a loaf of bread cost $0.16?

    a. 1953
    b. 1955
    c. 1957
    d. 1959

2. In this year, Disneyland Park in California opened:

    a. 1954
    b. 1955
    c. 1956
    d. 1957

3. Both Alaska and Hawaii earned statehood the same year that "Inca Silver" lacquer was offered. What year was it?

    a. 1958
    b. 1959
    c. 1960
    d. 1961

4. The novel *To Kill a Mockingbird* and Corvette's first race at 24 Hours of Le Mans occurred in which year?

   a. 1958
   b. 1959
   c. 1960
   d. 1961

5. What major event did not occur in 1963, when the rare Grand Sport was created?

   a. The Vietnam War started
   b. Assassination of President John F. Kennedy
   c. The first woman in space, Valentia Tershkova
   d. First successful lung transplant

6. In 1968, Corvette produced their fastest vehicle, and *this song* was a top hit of the year.

   a. "Brown Eyed Girl" – Van Morrison
   b. "Like a Rolling Stone" – Bob Dylan
   c. "California Dreamin'" – The Mamas & the Papas
   d. "Hey Jude" – The Beatles

7. In this year, Corvette saw the lowest number of Corvette sales and the Apollo 13 mission failure occurred.

   a. 1968
   b. 1970
   c. 1972
   d. 1974

8. What year saw the price of this Corvette at $6,810 and the end of the Vietnam War?

   a. 1970
   b. 1972
   c. 1975
   d. 1977

9. In this year, the highest number of Corvettes were sold while Black and Decker created their famous vacuum, The Dustbuster!

   a. 1979
   b. 1981
   c. 1983
   d. 1987

10. In this year no Corvettes were produced, and M*A*S*H aired its final episode with 125 million people watching.

    a. 1981
    b. 1983
    c. 1985
    d. 1987

11. This year would have the highest model of stolen Corvettes, and Ronald Reagan would be reelected for a second presidential term.

    a. 1979
    b. 1982
    c. 1984
    d. 1988

12. What year saw the "Copper Metallic" Corvette and the Chernobyl Disaster in Ukraine?

    a. 1986
    b. 1987
    c. 1988
    d. 1989

13. In this year, Corvette wanted to produce their fastest vehicle, and the popular film *Home Alone* also came out.

    a. 1989
    b. 1990
    c. 1991
    d. 1992

14. What event *didn't occur* in 1997 when the new C5 Corvette generation was released?

    a. Princess Diana died in a car accident.
    b. The film *Titanic* was released.
    c. The *Harry Potter and the Sorcerer's Stone* book was released.
    d. Bill Clinton began his presidential impeachment trial.

15. In what year did Corvette Race begin, and the world feared the Y2K computer bug?

    a. 1998
    b. 1999
    c. 2000
    d. 2001

16. Corvette introduced key-less start the same year Hurricane Katrina hit the Southern US. What year?
    a. 2005
    b. 2007
    c. 2009
    d. 2011

17. During this year, Corvette Racing saw 12 wins, and *Time Magazine* called the iPhone "Invention of the Year."
    a. 2000
    b. 2003
    c. 2005
    d. 2007

18. The first Corvette surpassed $100,000 in price and President Barak Obama was inaugurated in this year.
    a. 2008
    b. 2009
    c. 2010
    d. 2011

19. This year saw the re-introduction of Stingray and "Happy" by Pharrell Williams as top song.
    a. 2010
    b. 2014
    c. 2017
    d. 2016

20. What year did Corvette debut their first mid-engine vehicle?

   a. 2016
   b. 2017
   c. 2018
   d. 2019

21. The COVID-19 pandemic affected the world when the newest generation Corvette was introduced. What year?

   a. 2018
   b. 2019
   c. 2020
   d. 2021

ANSWERS

1. A – 1953
2. B – 1955
3. B – 1959
4. C – 1960
5. A – The Vietnam War started
6. D – "Hey Jude" – The Beatles
7. B – 1970
8. C – 1975
9. A – 1979
10. B – 1983
11. C – 1984
12. A – 1986
13. B – 1990
14. D – Bill Clinton began his presidential impeachment trial.
15. B – 1999
16. A – 2005
17. D – 2007
18. A – 2008

19. B – 2014

20. D - 2019

21. C – 2020

DID YOU KNOW?

- When the first Corvette was produced, the cost of a bread was 16 cents, while a gallon of milk was 94 cents! Another key thing during 1953 was that the average cost of a car was $1,800.

- Another iconic Corvette year was 1955. Another iconic thing created during this year was California's Disneyland!

- While Corvette was creating the LT2, which would be the fastest car they ever created, it was likely they were listening to the hit "Hey Jude" by the Beatles!

- 1975 marked the end of the Vietnam War, and saw the price of Corvettes reaching $6,810 for a coupe and $6,550 for a convertible!

- 53,807 units of the iconic C3 Corvette were sold, making it the highest selling years! During this same year, Black and Decker released their famous Dustbuster mini cordless vacuum! It is likely that Corvette owners would use this vacuum to keep their Corvettes clean!

- While 125 million people were watching the series finale of M*A*S*H, only a few 1983 Corvettes were created– with only one 1983 Corvette saved.

- In 1986, Corvette introduced the "copper metallic" version of the 305 V8 engine following critics claiming that the car was lackluster. Only four of these Corvettes were made; it was a new test color and only four owners chose it. There were quality issues, and they continued the color the following year with 87 more.

- The Corvette ZR-1 was created in 1990 with hopes that it could claim the title of fastest car. The car had 380 hp and reached 0-60 mph in 4.5 seconds with a top speed of 175 mph!

- In 1997, Corvette would create its 5th generation of Corvettes. Important social events also occurred this year, including the death of Princess Diana and the release of famed movie *Titanic*!

- While "Happy" by Pharrell Williams was playing on the radio as top song, Corvette re-introduced their iconic Stingray vehicle with a change in the name– one word rather than two!

- In 2019, Corvette debuted their first ever mid-engine Corvette. This revolutionary Corvette went for sale in 2020. With 6.2-liter LT2 V-8 engines, this car has 495 horsepower and can reach 0-60 mph in 2.8 seconds!

CHAPTER 18:
US ROAD FACTS

TRIVIA TIME!

1. What side of the car is the steering wheel located in the US?

    a. Left
    b. Right

2. True or False: You can pass a school bus with its flashing red lights on.

3. How many miles of road does the US have?

    a. 153 million miles
    b. 203 million miles
    c. 253 million miles
    d. 303 million miles

4. What lane is the passing lane?

    a. Right Lane
    b. Left Lane
    c. Center Lane

5. What city has an upside-down traffic light– green on the top, and red on the bottom?

   a. Philadelphia, Pennsylvania
   b. Springfield, Massachusetts
   c. Trenton, New Jersey
   d. Syracuse, New York

6. How fast is the highest legal speed limit in the US?

   a. 70 miles per hour
   b. 75 miles per hour
   c. 80 miles per hour
   d. 85 miles per hour

7. In what US state is "Santa Claus Lane" located?

   a. Alaska
   b. New York
   c. Washington
   d. Maine

8. True or False: Stop signs were originally called "Boulevard Stops."

9. What US interstate highway is the longest?

   a. I-95
   b. I-81
   c. I-90
   d. I-5

10. Where the longest street in the US located?

    a. Arizona
    b. Colorado
    c. Utah
    d. Montana

11. How long is the shortest street in the United States?

    a. 20 feet
    b. 520 feet
    c. 1,000 feet
    d. 1 mile

12. True or False: One mile of every five on an interstate must be straight so a plane can land in an emergency.

13. What is the most common street name?

    a. Main Street
    b. First Street
    c. Second street
    d. Third Street

14. What year was the Federal-Aid Highway Act passed?

    a. 1953
    b. 1954
    c. 1955
    d. 1956

15. What is the deadliest road in the Unites States?

   a. I-95
   b. I-15
   c. I-81
   d. I-05

16. Interstate: I-405 has the highest rate of vehicles per day. How many?

   a. 374,000
   b. 394,000
   c. 514,000
   d. 534,000

17. True or False: The color green was chosen for Interstate Highway signs based on a poll.

18. What year was the first centerline painted on roads?

   a. 1917
   b. 1927
   c. 1937
   d. 1947

19. Why were traffic lights invented?

   a. Dangerous intersections
   b. Police officers were nearly run over.
   c. It was hard to drive at night.
   d. To help with traffic

20. How many tires have been destroyed by the "nation's biggest pothole" on 1-75 near Detroit, Michigan?

    a. 5
    b. 15
    c. 25
    d. 35

ANSWERS

1. A – Left
2. False
3. C – 253 million miles
4. B - Left
5. D – Syracuse, New York
6. D – 85 miles per hour
7. A – Alaska
8. True
9. C – I-90
10. B – Colorado
11. A – 20 feet
12. False
13. C – Second Street
14. D - 1956
15. B – I-15
16. A – 374,000
17. True
18. A – 1917
19. B – Police officers were nearly being run over.
20. C – 25 tires

DID YOU KNOW?

- When driving through Syracuse, New York, be on lookout for the iconic upside-down traffic light! Located in the Irish neighborhood, it's the only traffic light in the country like it, created to pay respect to the Irish settlers in the area, with the Irish green on top!

- In "The North Pole," Alaska (yes, it's actually The North Pole) visitors can drive down Santa Claus Lane!

- Between Austin and San Antonio, Texas, the speed limit was changed to the fastest limit in the US at 85 miles per hour! The toll road between the two cities is 41 miles long and it will only take 29 minutes to reach them with the new speed!

- Interstate 90 is the longest highway in the United States, covering over 3,000 miles and stretching between Boston, Massachusetts, and ending near Seattle, Washington. The highway passes through 13 states, while I-95 passes through 15 states!

- The longest street in the US is located in Denver, Colorado– Colfax Avenue is 26.5 miles of a continuous street!

- Located in Bellefontaine, Ohio, McKinley Street is the "World's Shortest Street." The street is only 20 feet and McKinley Street earns its name from US President William McKinley!

- Following the US Census, it was discovered that Second Street was the most popular name, which went against the ideas that Main or First street would be the most common. Those two streets are actually 7th (Main) and 3rd (First) on the list.

- President Eisenhower passed the Federal-Aid Highway Act in 1956, which gave funding to create highways across the US. Without this act, the US might not have the 46,876 miles of roads that connects the county.

- Interstate Highway 15 that connects San Bernardino, California, and Las Vegas, Nevada is deemed the deadliest road in the US. In 2018, there were 128 traffic related deaths on the highway; the intense heat and lack of attention are some of the reasons behind the high number.

- The urban legend that surrounds the notion that one in five miles of Interstate Highways have to be straight for emergency plane lands is false. Highways were not designed for emergency plane landings, even though it has occurred before.

- In the 1950s, different colored Interstate signs were placed along the highways. Drivers would vote on their favorite colors– green won at 58 percent, blue with 27 percent, and black at 15 percent!

- It was determined that lines were needed to keep drivers on roads and not veer onto the opposite side. In 1917, designer Edward Hines was inspired by seeing spilled milk on the road, thus the white center line was created.

- In 1935, states were given the option of what color to use. By 1955, 49 states chose white paint with Oregon being the outlier, claiming that yellow was safer. The federal government threated to withhold $300 million of funding if the state didn't change to white. Yet, in 1971, the federal government changed and mandated that center lines be yellow!

- Traffic lights were invented to protect police officers from being run over, as they had to direct traffic by hand and standing in the intersection. Officer Lester Wire created the traffic light out of a birdhouse in Salt Lake City, Utah, in 1912!

www.ingramcontent.com/pod-product-compliance
Lightning Source LLC
Chambersburg PA
CBHW071445070526
44578CB00001B/223